Ready-Made Book Displays

Ready-Made Book Displays

Nancy M. Henkel

LIBRARIES UNLIMITED

AN IMPRINT OF ABC-CLIO, LLC
Santa Barbara, California • Denver, Colorado • Oxford, England

Library of Congress Cataloging-in-Publication Data

Henkel, Nancy M.
  Ready-made book displays / Nancy M. Henkel.
    p. cm.
  Includes bibliographical references and index.
  ISBN 978-1-59884-862-5 (pbk. : alk. paper) 1. Library exhibits. I.
Title.
  Z717.H46 2011
  021.7--dc23   2011017224

ISBN: 978-1-59884-862-5

15 14 13 12 11   1 2 3 4 5

Libraries Unlimited
An Imprint of ABC-CLIO, LLC

ABC-CLIO, LLC
130 Cremona Drive, P.O. Box 1911
Santa Barbara, California 93116-1911

This book is printed on acid-free paper ∞
Manufactured in the United States of America

Contents

Introduction

A friend at a neighboring library says that successful library programs are all about "butts in seats." The more people sitting in the chairs at an event, the more successful it is.

My philosophy for book displays is similar. It's all about "books out the door." A successful book display increases checkouts at my library. Yes, it should be attractive and thought-provoking and informative, and even a simple form of readers' advisory. But ultimately, success for me comes down to circulation. At their core, displays are for getting books out the door.

I've done hundreds of displays over the years, and this book is designed to bring some of the most successful and easy-to-replicate ones together in one place. The display themes can be used as is or as springboards for your own creativity.

If you already do displays, you know that you can spend lots of time and money to create striking and interesting displays. You can also just grab an armful of books and slap them between two crusty bookends at the circ desk.

The interesting thing I've discovered is that both types of display increase my circulation. I can spend a few hours to create a lovely display of cozy mysteries decorated with doilies and teapots and lamps with lace-covered shades, and patrons will check out those books. But I can also spend ten minutes and put out a stack of cozies with a nice sign in an acrylic holder and patrons will check out those as well. People will often check out an item just because you've called their attention to it.

I'm not saying it is bad or a waste of time to do complicated displays. However, if that isn't your forte or it isn't in your budget, you can still do quick and easy displays that get your collection moving. Display marketing works, and if you don't believe me, see how often you buy something off an endcap display at the grocery store. Often, those items are not even on sale, they are just on display. The grocer has simply drawn your attention to the item, and you bought it.

Another favorite tactic of grocers is to put up massive displays with themes such as "holiday baking" or "big game day." They use a well-traveled area to promote all manner of items that you can buy to stock your pantry, often without discounting the price. In fact, most retailers use this strategy just to get your attention: put a stack of any item (jeans, bath towels, boxes of lightbulbs) in the customer's path, and sellers know somebody will buy some of those items, on sale or not. Librarians can use the same logic: draw patron attention to something, and they will likely check it out.

All of the display themes in this book are for fiction titles, many of them concrete topics such as westerns, science fiction, or romantic suspense. I've just given them snazzy titles so patrons think they are reading something new. However, many of the displays are themed on esoteric properties, such as the words in the title or the cover art. For example, one of my favorite displays is called "Back in Circulation," and it comprises books with women's backs as the cover art. I've done a similar one with chairs, feet, and eyeballs. There is nothing similar about the books at all, except the picture on the front. This is where your readers' advisory skills come into play: use displays to bring together seemingly unrelated titles and even multiple formats that patrons would not have discovered on their own.

For each of the displays in this book, there is either a photo of a complete display or a detail photo showing part of the display. There is also a list of suggested props, a related Dewey subject list, a section for your notes about displays you create, a reproducible booklist, and, when appropriate, a related media list. One caveat about booklists that are based on the cover art: some of them may have a different cover in a newer edition, in paperback, or in audio. You may also notice that some of the books included do not have original copyright dates listed. This is simply because I have chosen to highlight a newer or more easily available edition.

Booklists are mostly recent titles that will probably be on the shelves of most public libraries or older titles that are classic or readily available. The lists can be used in two ways: as a starting place for you to fill your display inventory and as a reproducible list that patrons can take away with them. Booklists are adult titles only, but you could certainly find many teen and children's books that would contribute nicely to your displays.

There is also an appendix that suggests holidays and times of the year when particular displays would be appropriate. In addition, you will notice an extensive index. Titles with complete annotations included in this book are denoted in bold type. Titles with just a mention, but no annotation, are denoted in regular type.

Getting Started

If creating book displays is new to you or you are just looking for some new ideas, this section will help you get going. The best way to do that is to lay some groundwork about the philosophy of displays.

In the early and middle part of the twentieth century, a librarian in India named S. R. Ranganathan was very busy. He devoted his life to libraries and librarianship, and he created a book cataloging system called the Colon Classification Scheme. He also penned the "Five Laws of Library Science":

Books are for use.

Every reader, his or her book.

Every book, its reader.

Save the time of the reader.

The library is a growing organism.

These five laws serve as a philosophical basis for librarianship. I've always been fascinated by Ranganathan and by a theory that is still so relevant even after more than eighty years, so I decided to write the "Five Laws of Book Display." Like Ranganathan's laws, they provide a theoretical grounding for an important aspect of our work.

Five Laws of Book Display

Every book accessible.
Putting books in a locked display case or behind the staff counter doesn't increase your circulation. Tempt your patrons with great books and put them out where people can get at them.

It's not about the props.
Props can really enhance a display, but use them selectively. The display should be more about getting people to check out the books than it is about admiring the stuff displayed around them.

Every display has a theme.
Unite the items in the display under one theme, but orchestrate some serendipity into it. Combine fiction and nonfiction, use multiple formats, and add some books that are unexpected. A theme that resonates with patrons can be used over and over again.

Educate the reader.
Use themes that are timely, interesting and thought-provoking. The longer patrons stop and look, the more they will check out. When appropriate, include supplemental booklists or pathfinder information so the reader can pursue the topic further.

Location is everything.
Locate your displays near book shelves, checkout stations, reading areas, or where people are browsing or waiting. A good display is visible when patrons are already choosing books.

Once you have the philosophical grounding, you may need some concrete reasons as to why you should do displays, particularly if you have difficulty getting time off the desk for special projects. The main reasons to do displays are as follows.

Increase your circulation.

As mentioned in the introduction, displays are all about circulation. Books on display are more likely to circulate than books on a shelf. If you don't want your books to sit on a shelf, take them to a point of checkout and show them off.

Practice readers' advisory.

Readers' advisory is all about connecting people with books. Much of it happens when folks ask for your help finding a book. Unfortunately, some of our patrons never come to the service desk and never speak to a librarian. Use your displays as a way to share ideas for great books with your patrons, even if they won't come and ask you.

Give patrons a reason to come back.

Some libraries do displays as part of their regular routine. Patrons enjoy them and even come to expect them. Each time they visit the library, they detour to the display just to have a look at what you've got in it. Think of this as your version of the Macy's Christmas window display—people come every year just to see what they've done this season.

Highlight collections, programs, authors, etc.

Displays can be a great way to draw attention to a special collection you have in your building that patrons may not be aware of. They are also a great way to make a connection between your collection and any programs or author visits you may have coming up. This is just another great way to educate your patrons.

Create "I had no idea" moments.

There is a wonderful feeling that happens when someone walks past your display, sees something on it, and says, "Wow! I had no idea the library had books about . . ." Displays help you introduce your patrons to your collection specifically and to the wealth of items available in libraries in general.

Once you've decided to do displays, a main consideration is where you might position them so that they are most effective. The seven main places to situate a display are as follows.

Point of Checkout

This is right at your circulation desk or at your self-checkout machines, if you have them. This is like gum and candy at the grocery store: patrons are already checking out a book, why not just take another one? If your circ desk is cluttered with pencil holders, library card applications, and other miscellaneous items, brainstorm with your staff about ways to consolidate these items so you have a little space for books as well.

Endcap

Endcaps are another great place to put up displays because they are usually visible from a distance, located near browsing shelves, and they have a nice backing on which you can put up photos or other display decorations.

In Shelf

Because of space limitations, shelf displays usually can't be as elaborate as some of the other types of displays, but they can be just as effective. If patrons are wandering through your fiction shelves and find a book display waiting for them, they are likely to look at it and even take some books off of it.

Table Top

This is what I call display in-the-round. Patrons can see and approach it from all sides. Even a small table set in a well-traveled part of your library will be noticed and may encourage people to check out your materials.

Open Case

An open display case might be an actual display space, or it may just be a range of shelves that you've emptied out for that purpose. Although you probably won't be able to do much in the way of props, this is a great time to do a display based on cover art because the covers will be so prominently seen.

Windows

Window displays can be effective for drawing patrons into your library, for highlighting a specific collection, or for when you would like to use a valuable prop that would be vulnerable to theft if it were in a more open display. Window display cases are popular at mall libraries, and many school libraries have them as well.

Locked Display Case

In terms of increasing your circulation, this type of display is the least desirable. However, if you want to do an elaborate display with a lot of props, this is a good way to go. If you must lock up the books, try to have a table or a book cart nearby with copies that patrons can check out, or use color copies of the covers in the display rather than the actual books.

Once you have an idea about the what, why, and where of book displays, you need to start gathering ideas. An easy way to start is with the main fiction genres: fantasy, science fiction, western, mystery, and romance.

However, to make them more interesting, create a name for the display that generates a little excitement. For example, for a display of science fiction, call it "Boldly Go . . ." and include some Star Trek books to make a link with the display's title but you can include other SF titles as well. For a display of traditional westerns, call it "Louis L'Amour and More." The title makes a connection to an author with whom most people will be familiar and then introduces other authors that write similar books.

Another way to get ideas is to play off current events. In March during the running of the Iditarod, do a display about dog fiction and include nonfiction about the race such as *Winterdance* by Gary Paulsen. In December, I often do a display called "Season's Readings" with fiction about Christmas and other winter holidays. In May, I do a display of horse fiction to coincide with the Kentucky Derby. When a well-known author dies, I do a display of his or her work as well.

I also have a number of ready-made fliers with generic themes that can be used for quick displays. Examples of these include "Great Books, No Waiting," "I Love to Read," "Our Shelves Are Crowded," and "Have You Read . . .?" For these displays, just pull duplicate fiction titles or any books that make your shelves feel full. There isn't anything special about these books, but I've drawn patron attention to them, so they usually get checked out.

Other quick display ideas include:

"Think Globally, Read Locally"—a display of authors from your area

"Prize-Winning Fiction"—a display of books that have won various awards

"Books. Always in Good Taste"—a display of food fiction or cookbooks

"Walk a While in Someone Else's Shoes"—a display of biography or biographical fiction

"Truth Really Is Stranger than Fiction"—a display of books on odd topics

"Lavender, Mauve, Lilac"—a display of books with purple covers

Once you've done a display, take a photo of it and make a list of the books included so you don't have to reinvent the display the next time. You can also make a theme flier for displays that you do and keep them in a file. When you need an idea, simply flip through them to see what hasn't been done for a while.

You may also wish to keep a display log to track the effectiveness of particular displays. Include the name of the display, the number of books in the starting display inventory, the number of books that were checked out off the display, and the number of days the display was left up.

One year I kept an extremely careful log of displays at one specific checkout station so that I could prove what I believed anecdotally, which was that this particular spot made a great display space. That year I put up 27 displays for an average duration of 6 days. The total book display inventory for the year was 1,177 books, 952 of which were checked out, for an effectiveness rate of 80.88%. On page xiii is a sample log you can use to track the success of your own displays. It can be easily recreated as an Excel document to include the formulas.

Another step to successful displays is to involve your staff. This can be done in several ways. One is to make them aware of where you are putting up a display and what the theme is. Store your extra display inventory in a convenient place so that other staff members can fill in the display holes when you aren't there. You can also elicit ideas for displays from your staff and even invite them to be involved in the setup or inventory gathering. A school librarian once pointed out that students at her school are like her staff members and that they love to help with displays as well.

Something else to keep in mind about doing book displays is that you may have to educate your patrons about them. If you do a lot of displays in locked cases or behind a staff desk, put up a little sign letting people know they can ask for them. If you have an elaborate display with lots of props, you may find patrons unwilling to mess it up by taking something off of it. Vigilant monitoring of displays might be required for a bit until patrons realize that you actually want them to take the books.

A few other things to consider when creating displays are how you can add height or dimension to your displays to give them depth and add visual interest, how you can use color to enhance your theme or to better highlight your book covers, and how good placement can minimize how much of the "backstage" part of your display the patrons see. As you get more experienced with displays, these factors become even more important.

So, to sum up, the steps for creating displays are to pick your theme and your place, gather your inventory and any props you may be using, involve your staff with the maintenance, then photograph it, log it, and finally dismantle it. When people ask me what elements go into a great display, I always tell them that the best displays are cheap, quick to create, easy to maintain, and, most important, they are effective. If you follow the steps above, your displays will hopefully be all those things and much more.

Display Name	Inventory	Checkouts	Duration
Totals			
Efficiancy Percentage			
Average Days Per Display			

Adventure on the High Seas

"Call me Ishmael." One of the greatest opening lines in literature, this phrase alone can call to mind Melville's great tale of man versus whale, man versus the sea, and man versus his own ego. Stories set on the high seas are often some of the most fascinating, compelling, and passionate in the historical fiction genre.

Anchor this display with some of the great sea stories of all time such as Herman Melville's *Moby Dick*; *The Old Man and the Sea* by Ernest Hemingway; *Mutiny on the Bounty*, the first in Charles Nordhoff's archetypal trilogy; and of course the modern classic, Tom Clancy's *The Hunt for Red October*. Fill it in with any of the myriad series books set on the high seas by such authors as C. S. Forester, Dudley Pope, and Patrick O'Brian or the cruise ship mysteries by Conrad Allen.

This is a great display to coincide with the America's Cup races or, if you live on one of the coasts, local boat races and regattas.

Prop Ideas

Ship in a bottle

Nautical items (anchor, lifejacket)

Navigational equipment (sextant, compass)

Seashells

Plastic seaweed and fish

Related Dewey Subject List

Shipbuilding (623.82)

Navigational instruments (620.004 and 527)

Nautical history (387.5)

Shipwrecks (910.452)

Related Media

CDs of sea shanties

DVDs of sea films such as *Mutiny on the Bounty* starring Clark Gable or *Master and Commander* starring Russell Crowe

Notes

Booklist

Bernard Cornwell. *Sharpe's Trafalgar.* Perennial/HarperCollins, 2001.
> In this installment of Cornwell's best-selling series, British Army officer Richard Sharpe finds himself on a ship that is witness to Lord Nelson's bloody battle off Cape Trafalgar.

Clive Cussler. *Pacific Vortex!* Bantam, 1994.
> What's a nautical adventure list without Dirk Pitt? This time around, Cussler's famous NUMA agent is investigating a mysterious stretch of ocean that seems to have swallowed up a nuclear super-submarine.

John Drake. *Flint and Silver: A Prequel to Treasure Island.* Simon & Schuster, 2009.
> The title says it all. Drake imagines how Long John Silver lost his leg and how he became fast friends then bitter adversaries with Captain Flint. Swashbuckling, pirate shenanigans with some treachery, murder, and a runaway slave girl thrown in. This is the first in a series of books that takes place before the Robert Louis Stevenson classic.

Alexander Kent. *Colours Aloft!* McBooks Press, 2000.
> One in a long series of popular books about British Royal Navy officer Richard Bolitho, set during the Napoleonic Wars.

Dewey Lambdin. *A King's Commander.* McBooks Press, 2008.
> One in a series of novels about Alan Lewrie, a rather rakish, nontraditional British Naval captain who rises from the poorhouse in his infancy eventually to become a capable and respected officer.

Herman Melville. *Billy Budd.* Tor Classics, 1992.
> Often overshadowed by Melville's other little tome *Moby Dick*, this is the tragic story of a handsome young sailor loved by all save for the cruel master-at-arms who frames him for treason.

James L. Nelson. *Glory in the Name.* Morrow, 2003.
> Author of several nonfiction titles about early American Navy history, this time Nelson tells the story of the dramatic marine battles of the Civil War. This is the first of two books featuring Samuel Bowater and his tugboat-turned-Confederate-gunboat, *Cape Fear.*

Arturo Perez-Reverte. *The Nautical Chart.* Harcourt, 2001.
> Best known for his series about sword-for-hire Captain Diego Alatriste, Perez-Reverte takes to the sea for a story that combines suspense, love, and the search for a sunken treasure ship.

David Poyer. *Korea Strait.* St. Martin's Press, 2007.
> Seemingly ripped from the headlines, this thriller is one in the series featuring U.S. Navy captain Dan Lenson. This time he is chasing unidentified nuclear subs that may be an invasion force from North Korea.

Richard Woodman. *The Disastrous Voyage of the Santa Margarita.* Severn House, 2008.
> Mutiny! Typhoons! Scurvy! This story has all the elements of the worst sea voyage ever, and it is based on real events. Also check out Woodman's British Naval series featuring Nathaniel Drinkwater.

From *Ready-Made Book Displays* by Nancy M. Henkel. Santa Barbara, CA: Libraries Unlimited. Copyright © 2011.

Back in Circulation

This is a quirky idea that can easily work as a point-of-checkout, an in-shelf, or even a tabletop display. Similar to "Put Your Best Foot Forward" and "The Best Seat in the House," this display idea was born in the stacks. I was spending some time in fiction and came across at least three books that had women's backs on the cover. When I saw two others the next day, I knew I had the makings of an eye-catching display that didn't need much more than the book covers to make it work.

To easily increase your inventory, look at romance novels because the covers often include women's backs on them. The paranormal romance title *Butterfly Tattoo* by Deidre Knight shows a man's very muscular back with, naturally, a butterfly tattoo on it, so men's backs are also cover fodder. Clearly, the possibilities are very rich for this display.

Prop Ideas

Graphic depiction of a spine

Graphic depiction of back muscles

Spinal x-ray

Chiropractic spinal column in stand

Related Dewey Subject List

Back pain (617.564)

Pilates/stretching (613.71)

Notes

Booklist

Rhys Bowen. *In a Gilded Cage.* Minotaur Books, 2009.

    Bowen combines the suffrage movement, a flu epidemic, and the opium trade in this installment of the fun mystery series starring Irish immigrant Molly Murphy.

Nana Ekua Brew-Hammond. *Powder Necklace.* Washington Square Press, 2010.

    After she is sent by her mother to the family homeland of Ghana, London teenager Lila is next summoned to New York by her father. This is a coming-of-age and coming-to-your-roots story based loosely on the author's life.

Paulo Coelho. *Brida.* Harper, 2008.

    Brida O'Fern is a young Irish woman on a spiritual quest to find herself and her mystical destiny.

Dorothy Garlock. *Stay a Little Longer.* Grand Central Publishing, 2010.

    Post–World War I story about a midwife running her family's boarding house while fending off an evil banker and ultimately finding love in an unexpected place.

Susan Mallery. *The Seductive One.* Pocket Star Books, 2010.

    First in a romance trilogy about the Marcelli sisters, whose family owns a winery.

Anne Plantagenet. *Last Rendezvous.* Other Press, 2010.

    A vivid fictionalization of the life of French poet and actress Marceline Desbordes-Valmore.

Kate Quinn. *Mistress of Rome.* Berkley Books, 2010.

    A juicy tale set in ancient Rome about a slave named Thea who survives the siege of Masada and her spoiled nemesis Lepida.

Laura Joh Rowland. *The Fire Kimono.* Minotaur Books, 2008.

    One in a series of historical mysteries set in feudal Japan featuring the shogun's chamberlain, Sano Ichiro.

Tatjana Soli. *The Lotus Eaters.* St. Martin's Press, 2010.

    A fascinating debut novel about a female photographer trying to chronicle the Vietnam War.

Susan Wiggs. *Just Breathe.* Mira, 2008.

    When cartoonist Sarah Moon's husband wants a divorce, she heads cross-county to her hometown. Just as she begins her new life, she discovers she is pregnant with her ex's twins.

Best Seat in the House

Sometimes you see a book with a great cover and just know that you should build a display around it. However, cover art can be a challenging way to create a theme, and you may find only a few books with the right image. The next step is to find books with title words that connect to the theme.

When I was working on this display, I did a catalog search and found lots of books with the word "chair" in the title, but most of them didn't have chairs on the cover, and a large percentage of them were children's picture books. For my displays, I typically do a search crossing "fiction" with whatever my search term is, and it usually turns up enough for a decent-sized display inventory.

If you don't have much success with the word "chair," branch out and use words such as wheelchair, throne, bench, seat, and stool, and you can probably come up with enough books to make a display worthwhile.

To be honest, the real reason I wanted to do this display was so that I could use the set of mini chairs from Pottery Barn that you see in the display photo.

Prop Ideas

Chairs sized for Barbie or other dolls

Rocking chair or reading chair next to display

Related Dewey Subject List

Chair building (684.13)

Chair design (749.32)

Notes

Booklist

Caroline Adderson. *Sitting Practice*. Trumpeter, 2008.

     A dark yet funny novel about newlyweds whose lives change when the wife is paralyzed in an auto accident.

Joe Coomer. *One Vacant Chair*. Graywolf Press, 2003.

     Sarah and her aunt (a painter of chairs) travel to Scotland to fulfill her grandmother's dying wish.

Beth Kendrick. *Second Time Around*. Bantam Books, 2010.

     At their college reunion, four classmates discover that an old friend died and left them a huge inheritance. The catch is that each must use the money to re-create herself.

Sue Monk Kidd. *The Mermaid Chair*. Viking, 2005.

     On tiny Egret Island off the coast of South Carolina, Jessie Sullivan visits a monastery and is drawn to a monk about to take his final vows and to a beautiful chair dedicated to a mermaid who became a saint.

Celine Kiernan. *The Poison Throne*. Orbit, 2008.

     The first book in the fantasy series the <u>Moorehawke Trilogy</u>, about young Wynter Moorehawke who returns home to find the royal court torn apart by a terrible secret.

Chris Kuzneski. *The Lost Throne*. G. P. Putnam's Sons, 2009.

     Payne and Jones are top-secret, freelance agents who use their special forces training to investigate dangerous situations. This fast-moving adventure has lost treasure, religious artifacts, and deadly assassins.

John Lescroart. *The Second Chair*. Dutton, 2004.

     One of Lescroart's best-selling titles featuring disillusioned lawyer Dismas Hardy. This time around, he's sitting second chair in the trial of a teenager from a prominent family who is accused of murdering his girlfriend.

Jennifer Stevenson. *The Velvet Chair*. Del Rey, 2008.

     One in a series of sexy romances with a spunky heroine and a 200-year-old demon who investigate paranormal mysteries.

Anne Tyler. *The Accidental Tourist*. Ballantine Books, 2002.

     A tender, funny novel about a travel writer who hates to travel and the eccentric dog trainer who brings him out of his shell.

Valerie Wolzien. *Death in a Beach Chair*. Fawcett Books, 2004.

     Susan Henshaw, an amateur sleuth who loves to shop, must solve the murder of her friend's ex-sister-in-law while vacationing in the Caribbean.

Biblical Proportions

Inspirational fiction booklists are very popular in my library. The lists include books with Christian themes written by such authors at Karen Kingsbury, Jan Karon, Beverly Lewis, and Lori Wick. There are also many books written by mainstream authors that are retellings of Bible stories or novels about people in the Bible that are of interest to these patrons. Good examples include the <u>Women of Genesis</u> series by Orson Scott Card and the <u>Christ the Lord</u> series by Anne Rice. You could also throw in some old favorites such as *Two from Galilee* by Marjorie Holmes, *How Far to Bethlehem?* by Norah Lofts, and *The Robe* by Lloyd C. Douglas, if you still have copies of these around.

With this display, keep the decorating very minimal and just use a nice display flyer to showcase it. I try to steer clear of making this a display about religion and more a display about how the Bible is the literary basis for a lot of fiction. I normally don't put Bibles in the display, but I have included A. J. Jacobs terrific book *The Year of Living Biblically.*

Prop Ideas

Palm frond

Rough-hewn fabric as drop cloth

Map of the Holy Land

Related Dewey Subject List

Bible atlases (220.91)

People of the Bible (220.95)

Plants of the Bible (220.85 or 635)

Travel guides to Jerusalem and the Holy Land (915.695)

Related Media

CDs of Gregorian chants

DVDs of films such as *The Ten Commandments* starring Charlton Heston and Mel Gibson's *The Passion of the Christ* starring Jim Caviezel

Notes

_____

_____

_____

_____

_____

_____

_____

_____

_____

_____

_____

Booklist

Anita Diamant. *The Red Tent.* Picador/St. Martin's Press, 2007.
>Although Dinah receives only minor recognition in Genesis, she comes alive as the only daughter of the four wives of Jacob in this novel about the sisterhood of the Old Testament.

India Edghill. *Delilah.* St. Martin's Press, 2009.
>In this complex and beautiful retelling of a familiar story, Samson and Delilah are much more than a long-haired giant and a scissors-wielding temptress.

Elissa Elliott. *Eve: A Novel of the First Woman.* Delacorte, 2009.
>Told from the point of view of both Eve and her daughters, this is the story of many firsts and how a family born in a garden survives in the outside world.

Eva Etzioni-Halevy. *The Garden of Ruth.* Plume, 2007.
>Osnath arrives in Bethlehem and discovers a scrap of parchment that hints at a secret about Ruth, wife of Boaz, that her grandchildren are eager to hide.

Ginger Garrett. *The Chosen: The Lost Diaries of Queen Esther.* David C. Cook, 2010.
>Esther was captured, taken from her family, and thrown into the harem of Xerxes, the Persian king. Soon she discovers a plot that could destroy her people.

Marek Halter. *Mary of Nazareth.* Crown Publishers, 2008.
>Halter, author of <u>The Canaan Trilogy</u> (*Sarah*, *Zipporah*, and *Lilah*), now creates a back story for perhaps the most famous woman in the Bible, Mary.

Brooks Hansen. *John the Baptizer: A Novel.* W.W. Norton, 2009.
>A complex and colorful retelling of the story of John the Baptist, from the moment his birth is foretold by the angel Gabriel to his grisly end.

Ki Longfellow. *The Secret Magdalene.* Crown Publishers, 2007.
>One of several retellings of the story of Mary Magdalene, this version imagines her privileged childhood in Jerusalem and her eventual partnership with Jesus.

Christopher Moore. *Lamb: The Gospel According to Biff, Christ's Childhood Pal.* Morrow/HarperCollins, 2002.
>The hilarious and irreverent version of Christ's early life as told by his best friend.

Anne Provoost. *In the Shadow of the Ark.* Berkley Books, 2006.
>Re Jana's father is a shipbuilder, and he settles the family in the shipyard of Noach. A richly told novel that is both hopeful and tragic.

Blood Types: Vampire Fiction for Every Taste

Vampires just don't seem to be going away. There are novels about funny vampires, sexy vampires, literary knockoff vampires, and terrifying vampires. Many, many authors write in the vampire genre, so gathering titles is probably going to be fast and easy. Some of these writers include MaryJanice Davidson, Laurell K. Hamilton, Charlaine Harris, Erin McCarthy, Anne Rice, and Chelsea Quinn Yarbro. And, of course, you can also include Bram Stoker. But there are also some stand-alone vampire novels and some that are written by novelists who just wanted to take their fangs on a test run.

This is an easy and popular display to do, especially around Halloween, and you can resurrect it every time a new *Twilight* movie comes out.

Prop Ideas

Bats

Vampire cape

Plastic fangs

Related Dewey Subject List

Vampire myth and lore (398.21)

History of Romania/Transylvania (949.8)

Vampire movie history (791.4309)

Related Media

DVDs of vampire movies such as *Dracula* starring Gary Oldman, the classic version starring Bela Lugosi, or *Interview with a Vampire* starring Tom Cruise

Notes

_____

_____

_____

_____

_____

_____

_____

_____

_____

_____

_____

_____

_____

_____

_____

Booklist

Dakota Cassidy. *Accidentally Dead.* Berkley Sensation, 2008.
    In this installment of Cassidy's paranormal romances, dental hygienist Nina is turned into a vampire when she's accidentally bitten on the job.

Christopher Farnsworth. *Blood Oath.* G. P. Putnam's Sons, 2010.
    Nathaniel Cade is the president's secret weapon: a vampire who secretly defends the United States against unnatural threats.

Michael Thomas Ford. *Jane Bites Back.* Ballantine Books, 2010.
    Elizabeth Jane Fairfax just happens to be Jane Austen incognito, just happens to own a bookshop, and just happens to be a 233-year-old vampire. She also wants to get her last manuscript published.

Seth Grahame-Smith. *Abraham Lincoln, Vampire Hunter.* Grand Central Publishing, 2010.
    Sure, our sixteenth president freed slaves and steered the United States through one of the most traumatic periods in our history. But did you also know he was a force for good against the undead?

Matt Haig. *The Radleys.* Free Press, 2010.
    A middle-class British couple raising their teenagers must deal with midlife crises, vegan diets, and the fact that they are vampires hiding in plain sight.

Susan Hubbard. *The Society of S.* Simon & Schuster, 2007.
    The first in Hubbard's <u>Ethical Vampire</u> series is a twist on the usual vampire story set in a world where vampires coexist with humans.

Louise Marley. *Mozart's Blood.* Kensington Books, 2010.
    Teresa is a soprano vampire who carries the memories of victims past—including those of Mozart. A brilliantly conceived and executed tale that spans four centuries.

Robin McKinley. *Sunshine.* Berkley Books, 2003.
    As the daughter of a sorcerer, Rae Seddon, known as Sunshine, is being recruited to become part of the Special Others Forces to combat a vampire takeover. Meanwhile, she is kidnapped by a group of vampires who intend to serve her up to their boss for dinner.

Terence Taylor. *Blood Pressure: A Vampire Testament.* St. Martin's Press, 2010.
    Clean Slate Global plots to rid the world of vampires, except for its own army of undead. With flashbacks to the Harlem Renaissance, performance art, romance, and a battle against cancer, this complex novel lives up to its prequel, *Bite Marks*.

David Wellington. *99 Coffins: A Historical Vampire Tale.* Three Rivers Press, 2007.
    As the survivor of a vicious vampire attack, Laura Caxton has no desire to tangle with them again. However, when an archaeological dig in Gettysburg unearths ninety-nine coffins containing dead vampires and one empty coffin, she goes on a deadly quest to find the missing vampire and save the town.

Boldly Go . . .

Although I'm not a huge prop person, sometimes an item just cries out to be put in a display. A number of years ago my husband's grandmother gave him a telephone shaped like the starship *Enterprise* from *Star Trek*. The receiver is the saucer section of the ship, and the ring sounds like the red alert signal. It is complete kitsch, but almost no one can walk past it without exclaiming, "Isn't that the *Enterprise*?"

For a display like this, you could include some of the *Star Trek* novelizations and book spin-offs that have been done by a number of authors, and you might also include DVDs of the movies or TV series if you happen to have any on the shelf. Another idea is to highlight other general science fiction novels, including classics such as *Hitchhiker's Guide to the Galaxy* by Douglas Adams, *Stranger in a Strange Land* by Robert Heinlein, *Fahrenheit 451* by Ray Bradbury, and *I, Robot* by Isaac Asimov.

Prop Ideas

Constellation map

Cutout stars (yellow paper or aluminum foil) glued on black paper

Star streamers

Star Trek memorabilia

Letters cut out of aluminum foil for the title

Related Dewey Subject List

Planet/astronomy books (523s)

Star Trek television show (791.4575)

Star Trek graphic novels

Related Media

CDs of *Star Trek* movie soundtrack

DVDs of *Star Trek* movies and television episodes

Ender series by Orson Scott Card in graphic novel

Notes

Booklist

Kevin J. Anderson. *The Last Days of Krypton*. HarperEntertainment, 2007.
 The intriguing and dramatic back story of the fall of Krypton as well as the love story of Superman's parents, the only people who understood their planet was dying.

Catherine Asaro. *Diamond Star*. Baen Books, 2009.
 Rising rock star Del may discover that his singing talent is not enough as he becomes entangled in the politics of several interstellar civilizations.

Greg Bear. *Anvil of Stars*. Orb Books, 2008.
 In *The Forge of Gods*, Bear chronicled the destruction of Earth by robots. In this sequel, a few surviving humans come back to seek revenge.

Orson Scott Card. *Enders' Game*. Tor, 1991.
 This classic won both the Hugo and the Nebula Awards. It is the story of a kid who just thought he was gaming when in reality, he was commanding a fleet that would save the Earth from alien destruction.

Alan Dean Foster. *Patrimony*. Del Rey/Ballantine, 2007.
 In this installment of Foster's wildly popular series, <u>Flinx</u>, along with his sidekick Pip, travels to an out-of-the-way planet to look for his real father.

William Gibson. *Neuromancer*. Ace Books, 2000.
 Originally published in 1984, this multiple-award-winning classic about a burned-out computer geek spawned an entire culture and still resonates with readers more than twenty-five years after its publication.

Elizabeth Moon. *Victory Conditions*. Del Rey, 2008.
 This classic military science fiction novel is the final volume in the series about Kylara Vatta, a space warrior with one last chance to destroy her enemies and restore her family's honor.

Kim Stanley Robinson. *Red Mars*. Bantam Books, 1993.
 The first of three award-winning novels that chronicles the saga of Mars and its colonization.

Neal Stephenson. *Anathem*. William Morrow, 2008.
 Raz, an "avout," has spent almost all of his nineteen years in a scholarly cloister dedicated to science and philosophy, but now he and his friends are being called on to save the "saeculars."

David Weber. *Mission of Honor*. Baen Books, 2010.
 In this installment of the popular military SF series, Honor Harrington, a space heroine by which all future space heroines will surely be measured, hopes to finally bring peace to her galaxy.

Books about Books

Books about books, manuscripts, libraries, and bookstores are always close to a librarian's heart. There are many series books out there to round out this display, including the cozy mysteries by Jo Dereske about small-town librarian Wilhelmina Zukas, John Dunning's mystery series about antiquarian book dealer Cliff Janeway, Lorna Barrett's books about a New Hampshire town full of used bookstores, and of course, Jasper Fforde's books about literary detective Thursday Next.

On this display you could also include books that provide recommended reading, such as the terrific <u>Book Lust</u> series by Nancy Pearl as well as collections of *Unshelved*, the comic strip about libraries written by Gene Ambaum and Bill Barnes. I once used old and antique-looking books as props for the display. I put them in an acrylic box and used it as a pillar for my theme flyer. If you are using a display case, you could use these books as risers for your display items.

This is a nice display to have up in April during National Library Week.

Prop Ideas

Bookends

Bookmarks

Old, rare/antique or interesting books

Related Dewey Subject List

History of books (002)

Book discussion group recommendations (028.55)

History of book printing (686.209)

History of libraries (027)

Rare book price guides (020.75)

Related Media List

Music CD *Public Library* by Jonathan Rundman

DVD of *National Treasure, Book of Secrets* starring Nicolas Cage

Notes

Booklist

Matt Bronleewe. *Illuminated*. Thomas Nelson, 2007.

    To save his son, rare book dealer August Adams must decode the secrets hidden in the illuminations of a trio of Gutenberg Bibles.

Geraldine Brooks. *People of the Book*. Viking, 2008.

    While in the process of preserving a rare Hebrew manuscript, Hanna Heath uncovers some intriguing artifacts hidden in the binding—artifacts that reveal much more than just the history of the manuscript itself.

Kate Carlisle. *Homicide in Hardcover*. Obsidian, 2009.

    The first of Carlisle's <u>Bibliophile Mysteries</u> in which book preservationist Brooklyn Wainwright discovers the key to solving her mentor's murder may lie in Goethe's *Faust*.

Sheridan Hay. *The Secret of Lost Things*. Doubleday, 2006.

    The search for a long-lost Melville manuscript is at the heart of this story about a young woman who arrives in New York and finds herself working in a rare book store.

Judith Koll Healey. *The Canterbury Papers*. William Morrow, 2004.

    Alais is sent to Canterbury Cathedral by her guardian, Queen Eleanor of Aquitaine, to retrieve a parcel of letters that could bring down the king of England.

William Martin. *The Lost Constitution*. Forge, 2007.

    The past and present collide when Peter Fallon, a rare book expert, discovers the existence of an annotated Constitution that could change the way our Bill of Rights is carried out. Politicians from both sides of the aisle want their hands on it, but Peter must find it and protect it.

Kathleen McGowan. *The Expected One*. Simon and Schuster, 2006.

    While researching a book, journalist Maureen Pascal uncovers information about a set of scrolls written by Mary Magdalene that chronicles her version of the New Testament. The sequel is called *The Book of Love*.

Matthew Pearl. *The Last Dickens*. Random House, 2009.

    Pearl is a master of the literary mystery genre. This time around, lost pages from Charles Dickens's last manuscript could hold the key to stopping a murderer.

Carlos Ruiz Zafon. *Shadow of the Wind*. Penguin Press, 2004.

    In post–World War II Barcelona, Daniel's father takes him to the Cemetery of Forgotten Books to choose one for which he will be responsible. Soon he discovers that someone is systematically destroying all the other books written by his chosen author.

Mitch Silver. *In Secret Service*. Touchstone, 2007.

    When Amy Greenberg opens her grandfather's safe deposit box, she finds a copy of an unfinished manuscript by Ian Fleming that is his true account of his spy work during the war. Now people on both sides of the Atlantic are after Amy and the manuscript.

From *Ready-Made Book Displays* by Nancy M. Henkel. Santa Barbara, CA: Libraries Unlimited. Copyright © 2011.

Books Color Our World

The idea for this particular display came about through the generosity of my library's local quilt group. Active as fundraisers through annual quilt sales, the group decided that they would also like to gift the library with a permanent quilt. They created a beautiful banner quilt that still hangs in the library to this day, but when it first arrived, it was the centerpiece for a display of quilting books. Since then I've used it to showcase fiction books with a color in the title.

The display could look really nice in a big wall space but could also be done as a point-of-checkout or tabletop display. The easiest way to fill this display is to do a catalog search crossing "fiction" with as many colors as you can think of. You could also include classics such as *The Scarlet Pimpernel* by Baroness Orczy and *The Color Purple* by Alice Walker, and even *The Hunt for Red October* by Tom Clancy. You are limited only by the color wheel.

Prop Ideas

Colored fabric as a drop cloth

Colored paper as background behind books

Color palate sheets for paint samples

Streamers, balloons, or other colorful decorations

Related Dewey Subject List

Color theory (535.6)

Color in art (751)

Painting (751.42)

Notes

_____

_____

_____

_____

_____

_____

_____

_____

_____

_____

_____

_____

_____

_____

_____

_____

_____

Booklist

Monica Ali. *Alentejo Blue.* Scribner, 2006.
> A set of stories that link together to paint a picture of the people who inhabit the little village of Mamarossa, Portugal.

Anthony Burgess. *A Clockwork Orange.* Norton, 1967.
> The cult classic about a dystopia in which violent teenagers rule the country. Even more frightening than the movie.

Laura Caldwell. *Red, White & Dead.* Mira, 2009.
> One of several novels starring red-headed Izzy McNeil, a former lawyer turned private investigator, whose cases always seem to land her in hot water.

Dixie Cash. *Our Red Hot Romance Is Leaving Me Blue.* Avon, 2010.
> The ghost of Justin's dead wife might be visiting his house and moving her stuff around. Sounds like a job for plucky sleuths Debbie Sue and Edwina, aka The Domestic Equalizers.

Robert Conroy. *Red Inferno: 1945.* Ballantine Books, 2010.
> In this alternate history, Conroy imagines what would have happened if the Russians and the United States had turned on each other during World War II.

Patricia Falvey. *The Yellow House.* Center Street, 2009.
> Eileen O'Neill is the central character in this novel about politics, religion, and love in Northern Ireland at the beginning of the twentieth century.

Zane Grey. *Riders of the Purple Sage.* Modern Library, 2002.
> The best-known of Grey's many novels, *Riders of the Purple Sage* is often credited with helping to shape the western fiction genre. It is the story of a woman who inherits a Utah ranch from her Mormon father.

Sally Koslow. *Little Pink Slips.* G. P. Putnam's Sons, 2007.
> A real guilty pleasure, this novel tells the story of a woman who rises to and falls from the job of magazine editor-in-chief.

Jay Lake. *Green.* Tor, 2009.
> A fantasy about politics and magic and an unforgettable young girl who stubbornly names herself "Green."

Martin Solaris. *Black Minutes.* Black Cat, 2010.
> Multiple stories converge as Mexican police officer Ramon Cabrera investigates the murder of a journalist who is writing a book about a decades-old serial killer. Police procedural meets magical realism meets haunting character study.

Books Give You Wings

There was a while when it felt like every new book that came into my library had a crow on the cover. I felt like the librarian equivalent of Tippi Hedren in *The Birds*. If you see film footage of me examining the new bookshelf during this time period, you're sure to see Alfred Hitchcock lurking somewhere in the stacks.

But besides the crow phenomenon, there are many other fiction titles with birds (particularly birds of prey) on the cover or in the title. When you do this display, you might include books on bird watching in your region, some of which even include CDs with birdsongs on them. To fill out your inventory, try a catalog search crossing "fiction" with birds such as eagle, hawk, sparrow, finch, robin, heron, and yes, even crow.

Prop Ideas

Bird cage

Bag of bird seed

Bird feeder

Stuffed or wooden birds

Stuffed cat hidden behind the feeder

Blue fabric or paper with cotton ball clouds

Related Dewey Subject List

Bird identification guides (598.2)

Bird watching manuals (598.07)

Bird house building/design (690.89)

Notes

Booklist

Ann Cleeves. *Raven Black*. Thomas Dunne Books, 2007.
Series debut about Inspector Jimmy Perez, who lives in the Shetland Islands off the north coast of Scotland. In this installment, a quiet village is unhinged by the discovery of a murdered teenage girl.

Nicholas Drayson. *A Guide to the Birds of East Africa*. Houghton Mifflin Company, 2008.
Two members of the East African Ornithological Society compete in a bird-watching contest, vying for the opportunity to ask the lovely Rose to the annual Hunt Ball.

Louise Erdrich. *A Plague of Doves*. HarperCollins, 2008.
An unsolved murder in the town of Pluto, North Dakota, haunts several generations of white and Ojibwa descendants.

Ken Hodgson. *Should an Eagle Fall*. Five Star, 2010.
When a rancher accidentally kills a bald eagle, he becomes the target of a radical environmentalist movement.

Brad Kessler. *Birds in Fall*. Scribner, 2006.
When a plane crashes off the coast of Nova Scotia, the survivors come together at an inn to mourn the tragedy.

Anne Lamott. *Imperfect Birds*. Riverhead Books, 2010.
Rosie's parents must confront their daughter's drug addiction as well as their own misplaced trust. Features some characters from Lamott's previous books.

Thomas Maltman. *The Night Birds*. Soho, 2007.
A complex story about a German immigrant family and the secret they hold about the Dakota Sioux tribe that were banished from the neighboring lands. Winner of the Spur Award.

Lindsay McKenna. *Dangerous Prey*. HQN, 2008.
A healing romance about an injured firefighter and her old friend who operates a rehabilitation center for birds of prey.

Wilbur Smith. *Eagle in the Sky*. St. Martin's Press, 2006.
A grand adventure/love story set against the backdrop of political turmoil in Israel and the wild paradise of Africa.

Clive Woodall. *One for Sorrow, Two for Joy*. Ace Books, 2005.
The epic story of a little robin named Kirrick who rallies the eagles and the owls in a fight against the evil magpies that would destroy their peaceful nests.

Books in Bloom

This is yet another display whose idea was born in the stacks. One day I was in fiction and I noticed at least three different books in one range with names of flowers in the title. When something like that happens, I just can't ignore it. It's clearly a sign that I should bring those books together for collection marketing purposes.

To find titles to fill this display, search your catalog for "fiction" combined with as many different kinds of flowers as you can think of: rose, lily, daisy, hyacinth, tulip, lilac, and even dandelion. You could also search under title words like "flower," "garden," and "bloom."

Some nice additions to the display include titles from Lauren Willig's charming spy series that begins with *The Secret History of the Pink Carnation* as well as books in the Flower Shop Mysteries series by Kate Collins with titles such as *Acts of Violets*. And, of course, there are all those Blossom Street books by Debbie Macomber as well.

Prop Ideas

Flower pots

Garden tools

Artificial flowers (singles or in an arrangement)

Bag of topsoil (for the truly brave or for those with a forgiving janitorial staff)

Related Dewey Subject List

Gardening (635)

Landscaping (712)

Floral arranging (745.92)

Related Media

DVD episodes of *People, Places, and Plants: The Gardening Show* featuring Roger and Paul or DVD of *Gardens of the World*, a tour hosted by Audrey Hepburn

Notes

_____

_____

_____

_____

_____

_____

_____

_____

_____

_____

_____

_____

_____

Booklist

Mindy Starns Clark. *The Trouble with Tulip.* Harvest House, 2005.
> Part of the <u>Smart Chicks Mystery</u> series, Jo Tulip is definitely a smart chick: she writes a household hints advice column, and she's an amateur sleuth.

Jennifer Donnelly. *The Winter Rose.* Hyperion, 2008.
> The continuation of Donnelly's earlier book *The Tea Rose* in which India Selwyn Jones goes against the advice of her medical school professors and sets up a clinic in London's East End.

Kristen Hannah. *Winter Garden.* St. Martin's Press, 2010.
> Grown sisters Meredith and Nina return home upon their father's sudden death and slowly unravel the story of their reticent mother's life in World War II Leningrad.

Fern Michaels. *Wildflowers.* HQN Books, 2010.
> A combination re-release of *Sea Gypsy* and *Golden Lasso*, two early novels by prolific romance author Fern Michaels.

James Patterson. *Violets Are Blue.* Little, Brown, 2001.
> In this creepy installment of the <u>Alex Cross</u> series, the police profiler delves into the dark underworld of vampire wannabes.

Marta Perry. *Rachel's Garden.* Berkley Books, 2010.
> When her husband, Ezra, dies suddenly, Rachel must rely on her Amish community, including Ezra's best friend, for support.

Jeanne Ray. *Julie and Romeo.* New American Library, 2003.
> Two rival family-owned flower shops will never be the same when the grown children of the households meet and fall in love. *Julie and Romeo Get Lucky* is the equally sweet and fun sequel.

Indu Sundaresan. *In the Convent of Little Flowers.* Atria Books, 2008.
> A collection of short stories in which women in India are caught between the modern world and the traditions that have shaped their culture.

Rebecca Wells. *Ya-Yas in Bloom.* HarperCollins, 2005.
> This joyful and hilarious continuation of *The Divine Secrets of the Ya-Ya Sisterhood* picks up right where Vivi, Teensy, Necie, and Caro left off and reveals the origin of this remarkable friendship.

Sheryl Woods. *Flowers on Main.* Mira, 2009.
> Part of the <u>Chesapeake Shores</u> series, this installment brings Bree's ex-boyfriend back into her life with a vengeance.

By the Numbers

Here is a display that is really easy to fill just by walking through your fiction shelves. There are many books that have numbers or ordinals in the title. There are also many authors who write a book series with numbers in the title: Janet Evanovich, Debbie Macomber, James Patterson, Tara Taylor Quinn, and Matthew Reilly, to name a few.

When you do this display, try to use titles that have the actual number in the title, rather than the number written out, because the numbers add a degree of visual appeal. You could also include some nonfiction books with numbers in the title such as the "1001" books (e.g., *1001 Wines You Must Taste Before You Die* and *1001 Movies You Must See Before You Die*).

Prop Ideas

Flashcards with colorful number or math problems

Calculator

Abacus

Related Dewey Subject List

Numbers/numeration (513.2)

Number theory (512.7)

Roman numerals (513.5)

Numerology (133.335)

Notes

Booklist

Nevada Barr. *13 ½: A Novel.* Vanguard Press, 2009.

In a big departure from her Anna Pigeon mysteries, Barr writes a dark psychological thriller about a woman who marries a man who may have a past connected to a string of child murders.

David Benioff. *The 25th Hour.* Carroll and Graf, 2000.

As he does in *City of Thieves*, Benioff compresses an astonishingly complex story into a very short period of time for his characters. In this book, Monty spends his last day with his friends before leaving for a prison term.

Bebe Moore Campbell. *72 Hour Hold.* Alfred A. Knopf, 2005.

Campbell weaves together an amazing tapestry of a novel involving a beautiful girl with bipolar disorder, her mother who owns a designer clothing store and gets her into an emergency intervention program, and the Underground Railroad.

Lee Child. *61 Hours.* Delacorte Press, 2010.

Jack Reacher is back in another countdown thriller. When a bus crash lands him in a small town in South Dakota, he meets the star witness in an upcoming drug trial. Unfortunately, a hired assassin would also like to meet this witness, and Jack has sixty-one hours to stop him.

Michael Connelly. *9 Dragons.* Little, Brown and Company, 2009.

When LAPD Detective Harry Bosch begins investigating a member of a Los Angeles–based Hong Kong triad, his daughter goes missing, and he goes to Hong Kong to get her back.

Adena Halpern. *29.* Simon & Schuster, 2010.

Lucy's grandmother is seventy-nine, going on twenty-nine, so it should be no surprise that on her birthday, the old woman's wish to be twenty-nine for a day is granted.

Stephen Hunter. *The 47th Samurai.* Simon & Schuster, 2007.

Vietnam Vet Bob Lee Swagger vows to return a Japanese sword to his father's Iwo Jima comrade. But when a modern-day samurai uses the sword to kill the man's family, Swagger seeks revenge.

Katherine Neville. *The Eight.* Ballantine Books, 2008

Set between two time periods, this historical mystery revolves around a chess set that, when assembled, offers the player limitless power.

Jodi Picoult. *Nineteen Minutes.* Atria Books, 2007.

Picoult takes on the horrific aftermath of a school shooting in which the mother of one of the witnesses happens to be the presiding judge when the case goes to trial.

Kathy Reichs. *206 Bones.* Scribner, 2009.

An episodic Tempe Brennan novel in which the forensic anthropologist tries to figure out where an autopsy went wrong, and also why and how she ended up being held captive in what feels very much like a coffin.

Curl Up with the Purrfect Book

This is a pretty easy display to pull together because there are tons of authors who write fiction series about cats. Rather than a title-based booklist, there's an annotated author list to help you fill out your inventory. This is another display that works with minimal props on a tabletop or at a point-of-checkout station. Put out a stuffed cat and a ball of yarn, and patrons get the idea. When I did the quick display in the photo, patrons got the idea so much that one of them stole the kitten. Luckily, the children's librarian whom I borrowed it from said it was her extra kitten and she wasn't upset.

This display can work any time of year, but you might put it up in June to tie in with the American Humane Society's Adopt-a-Cat Month or in February for National Cat Health Month. You might also include a copy of *Dewey: The Small-Town Library Cat Who Touched the World* by Vicki Myron.

Prop Ideas

Ball of yarn

Squeaky mouse or other cat toys

Basket with a stuffed cat

Fabric with cats on it for a drop cloth

Related Dewey Subject List

Cat breeds (636.8089)

Cat care (636.8083)

Training your cat (636.8088)

Naming your cat (929.97)

Notes

_____

_____

_____

_____

_____

_____

_____

_____

_____

_____

_____

_____

_____

_____

_____

Author List

Lydia Adamson
    A series about Alice Nestleton, a crime-solving cat-sitter

Marian Babson
    British-themed cozies with titles such as *To Catch a Cat* and *Only the Cat Knows*

Lillian Jackson Braun
    <u>The Cat Who</u> series starring Siamese cats Koko and Yum-Yum

Rita Mae Brown
    Series "cowritten" with the author's pet, Sneaky Pie, about a cat named Mrs. Murphy

Blaize Clement
    Cozy mystery series about cat-sitter Dixie Hemingway

Carole Nelson Douglas
    Mysteries starring black cat Midnight Louie

Rebecca M. Hale
    The <u>Cats and Curios Mysteries</u> about a woman and her cats who inherit an antique store

Miranda James
    <u>Cats in the Stacks</u> mysteries about a crime-solving librarian and his cat, Diesel

Shirley Rousseau Murphy
    Stars Joe Grey, a feline private investigator

Leann Sweeney
    The <u>Cats in Trouble</u> series stars quilter Jillian Hart and her three beloved cats.

Dear Diary

If you were ever tempted to break the lock on your older sister's diary and read it, here's the booklist for you. All of these books are done in diary format, and it seems to be perennially popular with patrons. My all-time favorite (so far) is Helen Fielding's *Bridget Jones's Diary*, but I also loved *The Adrian Mole Diaries* by Sue Townsend when I first read it as a teenager. To find these in your catalog you may want to try search terms such as "diary," "journal," and "epistolary."

Besides fiction titles written as diaries, there is an incredibly large number of published journals written by famous individuals such as Samuel Johnson, Samuel Pepys, and William Clark and Meriwether Lewis. And don't forget the most famous journal of all, *The Diary of a Young Girl* by Anne Frank.

Prop Ideas

Ornate pens or pencils

Blank sheets of writing paper

Diary pages (written on or blank)

Related Dewey Subject List

Journal writing (808.066)

Journal/bookmaking (686)

Notes

Booklist

Douglas Carlton Abrams. *The Lost Diary of Don Juan*. Atria Books, 2007.
>At the urging of his benefactor (and to refute the lies), Juan Tenorio pens a diary and reveals his adventures and his mastery of the art of passion.

Sherman Alexie. *The Absolutely True Diary of a Part-Time Indian*. Little, Brown, 2007.
>Alexie's National Book Award–winning story about Junior, who leaves the Spokane Indian reservation to attend a neighboring school and finds that the mascot is the only other Indian.

Sandra Dallas. *The Diary of Mattie Spenser*. St. Martin's Griffin, 1997.
>A diary found in an attic brings forth the story of a young woman who endures life on the Colorado frontier.

Louise Erdrich. *Shadow Tag*. Harper, 2010.
>A troubled marriage. A man who reads his wife's diary. A woman who writes a pseudo-diary for her husband to find as well as a real one for herself. Two children caught in the middle.

Jim Fergus. *One Thousand White Women: The Journals of May Dodd*. St. Martin's Press, 1998.
>After being unfairly committed to an insane asylum by her snobbish family, May agrees to participate in a secret government program designed to "civilize" Native American warriors by marrying them to white women.

Laurie Graham. *Gone with the Windsors*. HarperCollins, 2006.
>A diary written by Wallis Simpson's wealthy and completely clueless best friend, Maybell, chronicling the divorcee's pursuit of her prince.

Syrie James. *Secret Diaries of Charlotte Brontë*. Avon, 2009.
>Here's the diary of the author of *Jane Eyre* as she herself might have written it: her secluded, bookish sisters, her drug-addicted brother, and her secret love.

Allen C. Kupfer. *The Journal of Professor Abraham Van Helsing*. Forge, 2004.
>An English professor discovers diary fragments purportedly belonging to Bram Stoker's fictional vampire hunter from *Dracula*, Abraham Van Helsing.

Nancy E. Turner. *These is my Words: The Diary of Sarah Agnes Prine, 1881–1901*. HarperCollins, 1998.
>Twenty years in the life of an adventurous woman living in the Arizona Territory. Based on the author's family memoirs.

Kate Westbrook. *The Moneypenny Diaries*. Thomas Dunne Books, 2008.
>After years of keeping some of Britain's and James Bond's most secret secrets, Miss Moneypenny speaks at last.

Don't Judge a Book by Its Movie

The connection between books and their movie version is very strong. I've participated in several debates with my brother-in-law (a philosophy Ph.D. candidate who loves to argue) regarding whether a movie could ever surpass a book. I contend that several of the Harry Potter movies are better than several of the books, simply because the filmmakers were able to effectively consolidate the story. He argues that W. P. Kinsella's *Shoeless Joe* was ruined by the way its movie, *Field of Dreams*, substituted a fictional author for J. D. Salinger. The debate goes on.

If you've ever worked at the reference desk and had a student come in who needs to read a "classic" that has never been made into a movie, you will appreciate this display. Guess what? Almost all classics have been made into a movie at one time or another. That's one of the reasons they are classic: the story resonates through time and across formats.

Your library has probably done a variation of this display, and I've seen many titles for it: "From Page to Screen," "Books on the Big Screen," and "Read a Movie, Watch a Book!" Many libraries display the DVD of the movie together with the book. This is a great display to do at the end of February to coincide with the Oscars or in July to coincide with the release of summer blockbusters.

Prop Ideas

Popcorn boxes (available at grocery stores)

Movie-style candy boxes (Raisinettes, Junior Mints, etc.)

Metal movie reels

Director's clapper

Related Dewey Subject List

Movie making (791.43)

Movie trivia (791.43)

History of Hollywood (791.43 and 384.8)

Related Media

DVD version of the books on display

Notes

_____

_____

_____

_____

_____

_____

_____

Booklist

Pat Conroy. *The Prince of Tides.* Houghton Mifflin, 1986.
> Tom Wingo spends a summer with his sister's psychiatrist trying to unravel their troubled childhood and learning about the healing power of love. Movie stars Nick Nolte and Barbra Streisand.

Michael Crichton. *Jurassic Park.* Knopf, 1990.
> A wealthy entrepreneur builds a secret island populated with dinosaurs created from prehistoric dinosaur DNA. Movie stars Sam Neill, Laura Dern, and Jeff Goldblum.

Louis de Bernieres. *Corelli's Mandolin.* Vintage Books, 1994.
> During World War II, an Italian artillery garrison is set up on a tiny Greek island. When the tide of the war turns, however, the Italians must defend the island from a German invasion. Movie stars Nicholas Cage and Penelope Cruz.

John Grisham. *The Firm.* Doubleday, 1991.
> A Harvard Law School grad is horrified to discover that the prestigious law firm that hired him may be mired in murder and corruption. Movie stars Tom Cruise and Gene Hackman.

Thomas Harris. *The Silence of the Lambs.* St. Martin's Press, 1988.
> A criminally insane psychiatrist may hold the key to helping an FBI trainee understand a serial killer she is hunting. Movie stars Anthony Hopkins and Jodie Foster.

Nick Hornby. *About a Boy.* Riverhead Books, 1998.
> A confirmed British bachelor decides to start dating single mothers and is somehow adopted by a twelve-year-old boy. Movie starts Hugh Grant.

Cormac McCarthy. *The Road.* Vintage Books, 2006.
> After most of humanity is killed in an apocalypse, a father and son set out to survive together. Movie stars Viggo Mortensen.

Audrey Niffenegger. *The Time Traveler's Wife.* Harcourt, 2003.
> A love story about an artist and the man she loves, who just happens to involuntarily travel through time. Movie stars Rachel McAdams and Eric Bana.

Bernhard Schlink. *The Reader.* Pantheon Books, 1997.
> A German teen has a secret affair with an older woman who suddenly disappears. Years later he discovers she may have harbored a terrible secret past. Movie stars Kate Winslet and Ralph Fiennes.

Alice Sebold. *The Lovely Bones.* Little, Brown, 2002.
> After she is murdered, Susie Salmon watches from heaven as her family deals with their grief and her father decides to catch her killer. Movie stars Saoirse Ronan and Stanley Tucci.

Edible Fiction

If you haven't noticed the proliferation of mystery series devoted to food, you haven't been paying attention. Cozy mysteries about chefs, restaurants, caterers, bakers, and even Amish innkeepers are everywhere. In fact, there are so many that instead of doing a title-based booklist, I've done a series/author list instead.

This display can also be under the name "Culinary Capers" as well as "Read 'em and Eat" and expanded to include general food-related fiction such as *Chocolat* by Joanne Harris and *Comfort Food* by Kate Jacobs. Or you can use the display to correspond with the release of food-related movies such as *Julie and Julia, Cloudy with a Chance of Meatballs,* and *Eat, Pray, Love.*

Prop Ideas

Cooking utensils (spatulas, measuring cups, whisks, etc.)

Place setting (place mat, cutlery, etc.)

Blank recipe cards

"Staff Pick" recipes that can be photocopied for patrons to take

Related Dewey Subject List

Cookbooks (641)

Food memoir/food critics (641)

Food gardening (635)

Restaurant guidebooks (647.95)

Related Media

DVD episodes of television cooking shows, such as *Iron Chef, America's Test Kitchen, Barefoot Contessa*, or any of the other series on the Food Network.

Notes

Culinary Mystery Series List

Hemlock Falls Mysteries by Claudia Bishop
　　　Delightful sisters Meg and Sarah Qulliam own and operate the Hemlock Falls Inn in upstate New York. Titles include *Toast Mortem* (Berkley Prime Crime, 2010).

Cooking Class Mysteries by Miranda Bliss
　　　Light-hearted mysteries featuring Washington, D.C., area friends Annie and Eve. Titles include *Cooking Up Murder* (Berkley Publishing, 2006).

Chocoholic Mysteries by JoAnna Carl
　　　Mouth-watering mysteries featuring candy store manager/amateur sleuth Lee McKinney. Titles include *The Chocolate Pirate Plot* (Obsidian, 2010).

Candy Shop Mysteries by Sammi Carter
　　　Set in small-town Colorado, these mysteries feature candy shop owner Abby Shaw. Titles include *Goody Goody Gunshots* (Berkley Prime Crime, 2008).

Cackleberry Club Mysteries by Laura Childs
　　　Widows Suzanne, Petra, and Toni bond together to run the Cackleberry Club café and to solve mysteries. Titles include *Bedeviled Eggs* (Berkley Prime Crime, 2010).

Coffeehouse Mysteries by Cleo Coyle
　　　The Manhattan coffeehouse Village Blend sets the stage for these atmospheric mysteries written with coffee lovers in mind. Titles include *Murder Most Frothy* (Berkley Prime Crime, 2006).

Murder with Recipes Mysteries by Isis Crawford
　　　A popular series about two sisters who run a small-town bake shop and catering business. Titles include *A Catered Birthday Party* (Kensington, 2009).

Goldy Schulz Catering Mysteries by Diane Mott Davidson
　　　Suspenseful and fun mysteries featuring Colorado caterer Goldy Schulz. Titles include *Fatally Flaky* (William Morrow, 2009).

Culinary Mystery with Recipes series by Nancy Fairbanks
　　　Food writer Carolyn Blue travels, eats delicious food and writes about it while solving mysteries. Titles include *Bon Bon Voyage* (Berkley Prime Crime, 2006).

Hannah Swensen Mysteries by Joanne Fluke
　　　In Lake Eden, Minnesota, bakery owner Hannah Swensen cooks up delectable desserts and solves murders. Titles include *Devil's Food Cake Murder* (Kensington, 2011).

Pennsylvania Dutch Mystery with Recipes series by Tamar Myers
　　　Mennonite Magdalena Yoder runs the Penn-Dutch Inn but also seems to be in the thick of all mysterious doings in her Amish community. Titles include *Butter Safe than Sorry* (New American Library, 2010).

Angie Amalfi Mysteries series by Joanne Pence
　　　These fast-paced mysteries feature struggling chef Angie Amalfi as well as her family and friends as she tries to stabilize her career and solve mysteries. Titles include *Red Hot Murder* (Avon, 2006).

Elect to Read

When people ask me why I like being a librarian, I tell them that the library is one of the last three places in which you can see your Constitutional rights in living, breathing action. A courtroom is the second place. The third is a voting booth.

This is a timely display to do in November during a general election or during the February or late summer primaries. You can fill the display with fiction titles about candidates and elections.

However, during presidential elections, you can take your display a step further. Set up a book election and allow patrons to nominate their favorite books to be on a book ballot. Host a book caucus in which patrons can come and discuss their favorite books and post the nominated book covers on the wall so that people can pick their ballot representatives. During the week of the election, hand out ballots and ask people to vote for their favorite book.

Prop Ideas

Ballot box

Blank ballots

Campaign signs with book titles on them

Related Dewey Subject List

Election law (324.6)

Women's suffrage (324.6 and 305.42)

Presidential elections (324.9)

Notes

_____

_____

_____

_____

_____

_____

_____

_____

_____

_____

_____

_____

_____

_____

_____

_____

_____

_____

_____

Booklist

Ethan Canin. *America America.* Random House, 2008.
> A wealthy political family befriends a young man from a working-class background. As he rises to become an aide to a presidential candidate, he starts to question his place in the political web.

Vince Flynn. *Act of Treason.* Atria Books, 2006.
> The master of the political thriller, Flynn pens a story about a presidential candidate who may have won because of sympathy over his wife's murder. CIA operative Mitch Rapp investigates just who is behind this murder.

Laura Hayden. *America the Beautiful.* Tyndale House Publishers, 2008.
> Emily Benton might have what it takes to be the first woman president of the United States. A novel about faith, campaigns, and political ethics.

David Liss. *A Spectacle of Corruption.* Random House, 2004.
> Set against the backdrop of the first General Election in England in 1722 is the story of ex-boxer and "thief-taker" Benjamin Weaver who has been sentenced to hang for a murder he did not commit.

David Mizner. *Hartsburg, USA.* Bloomsbury, 2007.
> The election race between two vastly different school-board candidates in a small Ohio town garners national attention.

Stephanie Perry Moore. *Chasing Faith.* Kensington, 2007.
> Christian Ware, a Secret Service agent, finds that her faith in God is restored when she takes on the assignment of guarding an influential Black minister who is running for president.

Patrick Robinson. *Diamondhead.* Vanguard Press, 2009.
> The debut of a series featuring Navy SEAL Mack Bedford in which he believes a candidate for the presidency of France may be an international terrorist.

Joel C. Rosenberg. *Dead Heat.* Tyndale House Publishers, 2008.
> With the world already tense about a war in the Middle East, the Secret Service uncovers a terrorist plot to assassinate a presidential candidate.

Jess Walter. *Citizen Vince.* Regan Books, 2005.
> Vince Camden is a thief who ended up working in a doughnut shop in Spokane as part of the witness protection program. Set against the backdrop of the Carter-Reagan election, Vince digs into his civic duty in a darkly comic fashion.

Robert Penn Warren. *All the King's Men.* Harcourt, 2005.
> The 1947 Pulitzer Prize winner traces the rise and fall of a Southern governor and is still as politically relevant today as it was when it was written.

From *Ready-Made Book Displays* by Nancy M. Henkel. Santa Barbara, CA: Libraries Unlimited. Copyright © 2011.

Everything Equine

My library isn't far from a well-known horse-racing track, so a display of horse books is usually pretty popular. I often do this display to coincide with the opening of the racing season or in May for the Kentucky Derby.

As with books about cats and dogs, there are a number of authors who write horse stories, including Rita Mae Brown, Michele Scott, and, of course, Dick Francis. But there are also some great nonfiction horse books that you could add to your inventory, including *The Horse Boy* by Rupert Isaacson about a man whose autistic son is helped by a horse, *Horse Soldiers* by Doug Stanton about a group of Special Forces members who went to war in Afghanistan against the Taliban on horseback, and *Seabiscuit* by Laura Hillenbrand about the rise of an American race horse.

Prop Ideas

Horse-track race programs

Horse-race betting forms

Model horses

Horse tack (bridle, bits, curry comb, etc.)

Horseshoes

Related Dewey Subject List

Horses (636.1)

Horse racing (798.4)

Dressage (798.23)

Biographies of famous jockeys (Bill Shoemaker, etc.)

Notes

Booklist

Nicholas Evans. *The Horse Whisperer.* Delacorte Press, 1995.
> A wounded horse named Pilgrim is at the center of this novel about a "horse whisperer," a man who can charm wild horses, and possibly wounded people as well.

Molly Gloss. *The Hearts of Horses.* Houghton Mifflin, 2007.
> Gloss weaves together historical accounts of cowgirls to create her protagonist, Martha Lessen, a shy cowgirl who gets work on a ranch in Oregon during World War I.

Will Henry. *The Blue Mustang.* Leisure Books, 2009.
> A classic rerelease about a boy who vows revenge against his father's murderer, accompanied only by his trusted horse.

Elmer Kelton. *Other Men's Horses.* Forge, 2009.
> A young Texas Ranger is charged with bringing a murdering horse trader to justice. But all is not so simple in 1880s Texas, and there is always a showdown.

Cormac McCarthy. *All the Pretty Horses.* Knopf, 1992.
> The first novel of McCarthy's iconic <u>Border Trilogy</u>, which won the National Book Award in 1992. You saw the mediocre movie; now read the book.

John McEvoy. *Significant Seven.* Poisoned Pen Press, 2010.
> One of McEvoy's Jack Doyle mysteries that involves murder and, of course, horse racing.

Per Petterson. *Out Stealing Horses.* Graywolf Press, 2005.
> When Trond Sander retires to a remote cabin in Norway, a chance meeting with a neighbor brings back memories of a fateful summer when he was a reckless teen.

Jean Rabe. *The Finest Creation.* Tor, 2004.
> The first volume in Rabe's fantasy trilogy about horses who are gifted with telepathic powers.

Willy Vlautin. *Lean on Pete.* Harper Perennial, 2010.
> An aging race horse bound for slaughter becomes the companion of a teen who is running away to restart his life.

Jeannette Walls. *Half-Broke Horses: A True-Life Novel.* Scribner, 2009.
> Walls follows *The Glass Castle*, a memoir about her childhood, with a thrilling fictionalization about her grandmother, Lily Casey Smith.

The Eyes Have It

In case you didn't know, January is National Eye Care Month. What a perfect time for a display of books with eyes on the cover. I discovered this cover art theme in the fiction stacks when I noticed a lot of eyes on the spines. I started pulling them out and discovered that there were lots of eyes on the front covers as well. Some are sinister, some are seductive, and some just make for a compelling image that attracts the reader.

This is yet another display that doesn't require much in the way of props to be successful. You can print a generic vision chart from the Internet and post that as a backdrop behind the books. This works as a point-of-checkout display, but it might be most successful on an endcap. The impact of spotting an eye chart posted on the end of an aisle might draw a lot of patron attention to your display.

Prop Ideas

Vision chart

Eyeglasses

Sunglasses

"Funny nose" glasses

3D glasses

Related Dewey Subject List

Eyes/vision (612.84 and 573.88)

Eyeglasses (617.7522)

Optical illusions (152.148)

Notes

Booklist

James Scott Bell. *Deceived.* Zondervan, 2009.
>   A suspense thriller that includes a beautiful blonde, a couple of dead bodies, and a saddlebag full of diamonds.

Peter Carey. *His Illegal Self.* Alfred A. Knopf, 2008.
>   Che lives in isolation with his grandmother until his mother, a militant radical on the run, comes for him. Now this seven-year-old is on the run as well.

Jack Cavanaugh. *Death Watch.* Zondervan, 2005.
>   A TV reporter who usually covers fluff stumbles on the story of her career: terrorists are sending out death notices to unsuspecting individuals, and they are indeed dying.

Elizabeth Eslami. *Bone Worship.* Pegasus Books, 2010.
>   When Jasmine drops out of college just short of graduating, her Iranian father decides to arrange a marriage for her.

Karen Joy Fowler. *Wit's End.* G. P. Putnam's Sons, 2008.
>   After her father dies, Rima visits her estranged grandmother in an attempt to reconnect. While there she discovers that her grandmother is a popular mystery author and that Rima and her father are of great interest to readers.

Philip Margolin. *Sleeping Beauty.* HarperCollins, 2004.
>   A best-selling author's new book about a serial killer may provide a way for one of his potential victims to survive.

Michael Palmer. *Second Opinion.* St. Martin's Press, 2009.
>   A medical thriller about a doctor whose father was the victim of a hit-and-run accident. The only way he can communicate to her about what happened is through eyeblinks.

David Peace. *Tokyo Year Zero.* Alfred A. Knopf, 2007.
>   Tokyo Metropolitan Police Inspector Minami leads a team investigating the reign of a serial killer dubbed the "Japanese Bluebeard," all amidst the chaos of post–World War II Tokyo.

Leigh Russell. *Cut Short.* No Exit Press, 2009.
>   When recently promoted Detective Inspector Geraldine Steel ends up in the little British hamlet of Woolsmarch, she expects it to be quiet. She doesn't expect a killer.

Indu Sundaresan. *Splendor of Silence.* Atria Books, 2006.
>   Wounded from the fighting in Burma, U.S. Army Captain Sam Hawthorne arrives in the Indian state of Rudrakot to search for his missing brother.

Follow the Yellow Book Road

This display is as simple as it sounds. It's made up entirely of books with yellow covers. It works well to do this one on some kind of shelf that invites face-outs and to put them close together as though the books are pavers in the yellow brick road. It would also work as a tabletop display, especially with a yellow tablecloth or possibly some black fabric to set it off.

Another option for this display is to play off *The Wizard of Oz* connection. You could include books from the L. Frank Baum series about Oz, of which there are many that most patrons have probably never heard of, as well as props that relate to the film. If you go with this option, I'd recommend putting this display in a case. A pair of ruby slippers might be a tempting item for a thief.

An alternative to this display is "Have You Read Any Great Books Lately?" This display is made up of books with red covers or "Black and White and Read All Over," a display made with books that have black and white covers.

Prop Ideas

Yellow fabric or tablecloth

Wizard of Oz dolls/figurines

Wizard of Oz movie objects: ruby slippers, oil can, witch's hat, etc.

Related Dewey Subject List

Biographies of Frank Baum or of Judy Garland and other cast members

Wizard of Oz movie history (791.4372)

Kansas history or travel (978.1 or 917.78)

Tornados (551.553)

Related Media

DVD of *The Wizard of Oz* starring Judy Garland

Notes

_____

_____

_____

_____

_____

_____

_____

_____

Booklist

Linda Barnes. *Heart of the World.* St. Martin's Minotaur, 2006.
   One in a series about private investigator Carlotta Carlyle in which she tries to find Paolina, a teen who is almost a daughter to her and has mysteriously disappeared.

Carl Hiaasen. *Nature Girl.* Knopf, 2006.
   Hiaasen blends thriller and screwball comedy like nobody else, and this time around Honey Santana drags her ex, her son, and her stalker deep into the Florida Everglades.

Julie Kramer. *Stalking Susan.* Doubleday, 2008.
   In a race against time, TV reporter Riley Spartz stages an on-air event to reveal the identity of a serial killer who kills a woman named Susan on the same day every year.

Alexander McCall Smith. *The Lost Art of Gratitude.* Pantheon Books, 2009.
   This time around, the charmingly philosophizing sleuth Isabel Dalhausie tries to uncover whether Minty is running a fraudulent investment scheme.

G. A. McKevett. *Poisoned Tarts.* Kensington, 2007.
   It's murder in Hollywood on Halloween for plus-sized private investigator Savannah Reid.

Leslie Meier. *Mother's Day Murder.* Kensington, 2009.
   Lucy Stone, part-time reporter for the *Pennysaver* newspaper in Tinker's Cove, Maine, juggles subplots and political rivalry when a local teenager is murdered.

Tawni O'Dell. *Sister Mine.* Shaye Areheart Books, 2007.
   For eighteen years, Shae-Lynn believed her sister was dead, and during that time, she built a life for herself and her son in a Pennsylvania mining town. Then her world is turned upside down when her sister returns, bringing a cast of assorted characters with her.

Robert Rankin. *The Hollow Chocolate Bunnies of the Apocalypse.* Gollancz, 2003.
   Someone is murdering nursery rhyme characters! When Jack comes to Toy City to make his fortune, he teams up with a teddy bear detective named Eddie to solve the crimes.

Gemma Townley. *Learning Curves: A Novel of Sex, Suits, and Business Affairs.* Ballantine Books, 2006.
   British miss Jennifer Bell has divorced parents who run rival firms. When her mum asks her to spy on her dad, she isn't sure who to trust. On the other hand, she's sure she likes the handsome new guest lecturer in their MBA program.

Stephen White. *Kill Me.* Dutton, 2006.
   A medical, ethical, psychological thriller that asks readers to decide whether they would choose the time of their own deaths if they could.

Get One Third Off

This is a quick and easy display to do. Just go through and pull thin novels and put up a sign announcing that patrons get one-third off their books. Make the sign look like an advertisement, and print it in red with bright yellow letters. You could also make bookmarks that have "1/3 off" at the top and put them in some of the short novels on the shelf to draw attention to them.

This display works as a point-of-checkout display but also works as a shelf display. It is also fun to pair the books on this display with the ones in the "Get 25% off " display of long novels.

There are a number of authors who write mini-novels, so you can easily refill this display with their books. Some of these include Mitch Albom and Richard Paul Evans, and you could also include some short classics like *The Old Man and the Sea* by Ernest Hemingway and *The Great Gatsby* by F. Scott Fitzgerald.

Prop Ideas

Flyer to advertise the sale of short books

Bookmarks with "1/3 off" on them

Related Dewey Subject List

History and criticism of short stories (809.3)

Notes

Booklist

Sherman Alexie. *Flight.* Black Cat, 2007.

> A series of time travel events transforms an orphaned Native American teenager. A comic magical realism adventure.

Alan Bennett. *The Uncommon Reader.* Farrar, Straus & Giroux, 2007.

> When a bookmobile is parked outside Buckingham Palace, the queen checks out a book and discovers the joy of reading, which has some long-reaching repercussions for the British people.

Xiaolu Guo. *Twenty Fragments of a Ravenous Youth.* Nan A. Talese/Doubleday, 2008.

> A young woman leaves behind the sweet potato farm of her rural childhood to follow her dreams in Beijing. Guo paints a portrait of what it is like to be young, modern, and Chinese.

Colin Harrison. *Risk.* Picador, 2009.

> George Young, a lawyer for an insurance company, is asked by the firm's founder to investigate her son's mysterious, violent death.

Karen Kingsbury. *Hannah's Hope.* Warner Faith, 2005.

> The final volume in the <u>Red Gloves Collection</u> by prolific Christian author Karen Kingsbury. Hannah has a hazy memory of the man she thought was her father. Then the truth comes out and the entire state wants to help with a father-daughter reunion.

C. S. Richardson. *The End of the Alphabet.* Doubleday, 2007.

> A love story/travelogue about a man and his wife who find out he only has a month to live, so they embark on a whirlwind tour of places from A to Z that he has always wanted to visit.

Francine Rivers. *Unafraid.* Tyndale House, 2001.

> The culminating volume in the <u>Lineage of Grace</u> series about the female ancestors of Jesus. This book is the story of Mary, while others in the series have been about Ruth, Bathsheba, Rahab, and Tamar.

Sapphire. *Push.* Alfred A. Knopf, 1996.

> This title was rereleased under the name *Precious* to coincide with the movie premier. Tells the heartbreaking story of a Harlem teen who is unspeakably abused but ultimately rises above her circumstances.

Congwen Shen. *Border Town.* Harper Perennial, 2009.

> Originally published in 1934, this slim novel tells the story of a young woman and her grandfather who live in rural China and operate a river ferry near Chadong. Banned during the Mao era in China, this book has been reissued for a modern audience.

Dan Simmons. *Muse of Fire.* Subterranean Press, 2008.

> An interstellar group of players called Earth's Men travel the galaxy performing Shakespeare for human slaves on other planets, until they get the attention of the aliens.

Get 25 Percent More

This display is a great way to alleviate crowded shelves. Just go through and pull thick novels and put up a sign announcing that patrons get 25% more book for free. Make the sign look like an advertisement and print it in red with bright yellow letters. You could also make bookmarks that have "25% More Free" at the top and put them in some of the longer novels on the shelf to draw attention to them.

This display works as a point-of-checkout display but also as a shelf display. It is also fun to pair the books in this display with the ones from the "Get 1/3 off" display of short novels.

A number of authors write mega-novels, so you can easily refill this display with their books. Some of these include Diana Gabaldon, Robert Jordan, Stephen King, Wally Lamb, James Michener, and Edward Rutherford.

Prop Ideas

Flyer to advertise the free extra pages

Bookmarks with "25% more free" on them

Notes

_____

_____

_____

_____

_____

_____

_____

_____

_____

_____

_____

_____

_____

_____

_____

_____

_____

_____

_____

_____

_____

Booklist

Thomas Bertram Costain. *The Silver Chalice.* Loyola Press, 2006.
>This classic is about a young silversmith named Basil who is chosen to forge a holder for the cup that will be used by Jesus during the Last Supper.

Sara Donati. *Into the Wilderness.* Delta Trade, 2008.
>An epic historical romance in the tradition of Diana Gabaldon about a woman who leaves England in 1792 to rendezvous with her father in remote upstate New York. The first volume in a series.

Margaret George. *Helen of Troy.* Viking, 2005.
>Was hers the face that launched a thousand pages? Well, at least 600 are filled in this retelling of the Trojan War.

Jonathan Littell. *The Kindly Ones.* Harper, 2009.
>Max Aue, a former Nazi officer, lives quietly in France as a factory owner. In this fictionalized memoir, he looks back on the atrocities of the Holocaust and the part he played in them.

Colleen McCullough. *The First Man in Rome.* Avon Books, 2008.
>The first volume in McCullough's Masters of Rome series, which introduces the power and pageantry of the Roman Empire and two men determined to rule it.

Larry McMurtry. *Lonesome Dove.* Simon and Schuster, 2005.
>The Pulitzer Prize–winning epic about two cowboys, a cattle drive, and so much more.

Rosamund Pilcher. *Coming Home.* St. Martin's Press, 1996.
>A coming-of-age story about love and friendship that spans decades and continents.

Dan Simmons. *Drood.* Little, Brown and Company, 2009.
>Wilkie Collins narrates this gripping account of friend and fellow writer Charles Dickens's last years, and his last, unfinished novel.

Neal Stephenson. *Anathem.* William Morrow, 2008.
>Raz, an "avout," has spent almost all of his nineteen years in a scholarly cloister dedicated to science and philosophy, but now he and his friends are being called on to save the "saeculars."

Irving Stone. *The Agony and the Ecstasy.* Penguin Books, 1961.
>The life and loves of Renaissance man Michelangelo are chronicled, along with his artistic and political struggles.

From *Ready-Made Book Displays* by Nancy M. Henkel. Santa Barbara, CA: Libraries Unlimited. Copyright © 2011.

Grand Openings

"Where's Papa going with that ax?" A great opening line, like this one from E. B. White's children's classic, *Charlotte's Web*, sets the stage for a great novel, particularly if the author can maintain the momentum throughout the rest of the book.

To gather inventory for this display, your best bet is to go to your shelves and start opening books. You can't go wrong picking up classics like *A Tale of Two Cities* by Charles Dickens and Jane Austen's *Pride and Prejudice* for a terrific opener, but you can also check out first lines by some of your favorite authors. They don't necessarily have to be literary, they just have to be interesting. For example, one of my all-time favorite lines comes from another children's classic, Betty MacDonald's *Mrs. Piggle-Wiggle*: "I expect I might as well begin by telling you about Mrs. Piggle-Wiggle so that whenever I mention her name, which I do very often in this book, you will not interrupt and ask, 'Who is Mrs. Piggle-Wiggle?'"

An easy way to promote this display is to print a book's opening line and post it next to the book to draw patron attention.

Prop Ideas

Colored flags

"Grand Opening" signage

Famous first lines from well-known novels printed on note cards

Related Dewey Subject List

Book discussion group recommendations (028.55)

Opening a business (658.02)

Related Media

DVDs of books made from many of the books listed below are available.

Notes

_____

_____

_____

_____

_____

_____

_____

_____

_____

_____

_____

_____

_____

_____

_____

_____

Booklist

Isabel Allende. *Daughter of Fortune.* HarperCollins, 1999.
"Everyone is born with some special talent, and Eliza Sommers discovered early on that she had two: a good sense of smell and a good memory."

C. J. Box. *Savage Run.* G. P. Putnam's Sons, 2002.
"On the third day of their honeymoon, infamous environmental activist Stewie Woods and his new bride, Annabel Bellotti, were spiking trees in the Bighorn National Forest when a cow exploded and blew them up."

Willa Cather. *O Pioneers!* Bantam Books, 1989.
"One January day, thirty years ago, the little town of Hanover, anchored on a windy Nebraska tableland, was trying not to be blown away."

Earl Emerson. *Catfish Café.* Ballantine Publishing, 1998.
"Luther Little drove dead bodies around Seattle the way some people drove pizzas."

Carrie Fisher. *Postcards from the Edge.* Simon & Schuster, 1987.
"Maybe I shouldn't have given the guy who pumped my stomach my phone number, but who cares?"

Ken Follett. *Code to Zero.* Dutton, 2000.
"He woke up scared."

Gabriel Garcia Marquez. *Love in the Time of Cholera.* Vintage, 1988.
"It was inevitable: the scent of bitter almonds always reminded him of the fate of unrequited love."

Alice Hoffman. *Practical Magic.* Berkley Books, 1995.
"For more than two hundred years, the Owens women have been blamed for everything that has gone wrong in town."

Margaret Mitchell. *Gone with the Wind.* Scribner, 2007.
"Scarlett O'Hara was not beautiful . . ."

George Orwell. *1984.* New American Library, 1981.
"It was a bright cold day in April, and the clocks were striking thirteen."

Hard-Boiled Detectives

Mystery and detective stories are a perennial favorite among library patrons. And there is a subgenre for every reader: cozies, amateur or professional sleuths, police procedurals, suspense/thrillers, and the subject of this display, the hard-boiled detective. Now, there are lots of private investigator stories out there, but this display focuses on the noir aspect of the subgenre: the tough, gritty, and sometimes violent side of the detective world.

To gather inventory, you can always turn to the original masters in the field such as Dashiell Hammett, creator of the iconic Sam Spade, and Raymond Chandler, who brought us Philip Marlowe. But there are many other authors who have created this same caliber of detective. They are listed below, along with a few sample titles. Pair this with the "Tough Cookies" display, which highlights strong female fictional characters.

Finally, consider beefing up your display with movie versions of classic hard-boiled detectives like *The Maltese Falcon* or *The Big Sleep*, both with characters brought to life by a real-life icon, Humphrey Bogart.

Prop Ideas

Trench coat

Fedora

Folded newspaper

Prop gun

Copies of pulp magazines

Related Dewey Subject List

History of detective and mystery stories (813.08)

History of detective and mystery movies (791.430909)

Noir film (791.43655)

Notes

Hard-Boiled Detective Author List

Lawrence Block
> *Everybody Dies* and *Hope to Die* featuring alcoholic ex-cop Matthew Scudder who now works as an unlicensed private eye.

James Ellroy
> *Because the Night* and *Blood on the Moon* featuring brilliant LAPD Detective Sergeant Lloyd Hopkins who doesn't sleep while working on a case.

Loren Estleman
> *American Detective* and *Nicotine Kiss* featuring streetwise Amos Walker, a Detroit private detective and Vietnam vet, with a noir flavor.

Chester Himes
> *The Big Gold Dream* and *Blind Man with a Pistol* featuring tough, philosophical detective Grave Digger Jones and his partner Coffin Ed Johnson.

Stuart Kaminsky
> *Black Knight in Red Square* and *Blood and Rubies* featuring one-legged, post-Soviet Police Inspector Porfiry Rostnikov.

John D. MacDonald
> *Free Fall in Crimson* and *The Lonely Silver Rain* featuring "salvage consultant" Travis McGee who lives on a custom-made barge in Fort Lauderdale, Florida.

Ross MacDonald
> *The Goodbye Look* and *The Instant Enemy* featuring somewhat mysterious private detective Lew Archer who works the LA suburbs in the 1950s and 1960s.

Walter Mosley
> *Blond Faith* and *Devil in a Blue Dress* featuring World War II vet Easy Rawlins, a private investigator whose stories are part detective novel and part social commentary.

Robert B. Parker
> *Split Image* and *Night and Day* featuring fired LAPD homicide detective Jesse Stone who ends up police chief in small-town Massachusetts.

John Sandford
> *Silent Prey* and *Storm Prey* featuring maverick, tough-guy Minnesota investigator Lucas Davenport.

Mickey Spillane
> *The Big Bang* and *The Goliath Bone* featuring iconic Mike Hammer, the violent and cynical New York private investigator.

Rex Stout
> *Family Affair* and *The Doorbell Rang* featuring corpulent detective Nero Wolfe, who rarely leaves his luxurious Manhattan brownstone.

Here Comes the Bride

Usually when people do wedding displays, they focus on books about wedding planning and other appropriate sections of Dewey. However, there are a huge number of fiction titles about weddings, and adding those to a display brings an element of fun to the theme. Specifically, authors such as Nora Roberts and Debbie Macomber have bridal series books, and many romance novels have weddings as a central element.

This display works in February for National Marriage Week (February 7–14), as well as in the summer when a lot of weddings tend to happen. It can be done as a point-of-checkout display with just a simple flyer in an acrylic holder and a little statue of a bride and groom or as a big wall display with a veil, flowers, and even a unity candle.

Prop Ideas

Veil, white shoes or gloves, bridal hair ornaments, etc.

Bouquets, flowers, dried corsages, etc.

Hearts, ribbons, garland

White, gauzy fabric as drop cloth or background

Guest book, goblets, cake cutter, candles, etc.

Related Dewey Subject List

Honeymoon destinations (914–919)

Wedding cakes (641.8653)

Wedding decorations (745.5941)

Wedding flowers (745.926)

Wedding gowns (392.54 and 646.47)

Wedding music (782.434163)

Wedding photography (778.993925)

Wedding planning and etiquette (395.22)

Related Media

CDs with wedding songs

Notes

_____

_____

_____

_____

_____

_____

_____

_____

Booklist

C. A. Belmond. *A Rather Charming Invitation.* New American Library, 2010.
    The third book in Belmond's cozy <u>Rather</u> series. Amateur sleuths Penny and Jeremy may finally walk down the aisle if they can recover their antique bridal tapestry.

Robert Dalby. *Piggly Wiggly Wedding.* G. P. Putnam's Sons, 2009.
    The seventy-something mayor of Second Creek, Mississippi, Hale "Mr. Choppy" Dunbar, has finally convinced the love of his life, Gaylie Girl Lyons, to marry him. With the help of the "Nitwits," it just might happen.

Jodi Della Femina. *By Invitation Only.* St. Martin's Press, 2009.
    A summer wedding in the Hamptons has all the elements you would expect: great food, snobby bridesmaids, and a raging mother-in-law.

Katie Fforde. *Wedding Season.* St. Martin's Press, 2010.
    A London wedding planner doesn't believe in love. Neither do her two best friends. They are wrong.

Tate Hallaway. *Dead If I Do.* Berkley Books, 2009.
    Garnet and her vampire boyfriend are about to get hitched, if his vampire-zombie ex-girlfriend doesn't get in the way.

Gemma Halliday. *Mayhem in High Heels.* Making It, 2009.
    One in a series of funny, romantic mysteries about shoe designer Maddie Springer in which she is finally getting married but her wedding planner ends up dead.

James Patterson. *Cross Fire.* Little, Brown and Company, 2010.
    Psychopaths and corruption are all in a day's work for detective Alex Cross—even as he and Bree plan their wedding.

Denise Swanson. *Murder of a Wedding Belle.* Obsidian, 2010.
    A fun addition to the <u>Scrumble River</u> mysteries. In this one, Skye has to solve the mystery of the wedding planner's murder *and* help her cousin get to the church on time.

Ayelet Waldman. *Red Hook Road.* Doubleday, 2010.
    A tragic accident kills two newlyweds on their wedding day, and their families are left to pick up the pieces over the course of the next four summers as they celebrate the couple's anniversary.

Susan Wiggs, Sherryl Woods, and Susan Mallery. *Summer Brides.* Mira, 2010.
    A trio of wedding-themed novellas by three powerhouse romance novelists.

High Octane Thrillers

I had a professor in my undergraduate days who often referred to a nebulous genre of fiction he termed "male escape literature." To him these were books that guys read with a beer in one hand and the other hand stuffed inside a bag of chips. He felt that there was an entire category of books that only men read and that they did it to escape the doldrums of their lives, which explains why the books always had lots of action and explosions.

When I became a librarian, I learned a few things. One is that if patrons read while eating potato chips, the pages get greasy, and the other is that it isn't just men that like "male escape literature." I've had plenty of women over the years who've read everything by such authors as James Patterson and Ridley Pearson, and they wanted more. Maybe women want a few explosions in their books just as much as men do.

Here's a display that doesn't need much ornamentation, although once I did a tabletop display on this topic that played on the explosion theme. I put an open briefcase in the center of the display with a clock in it and wires coming out. The wires were attached to a piece of circuitry from an old computer motherboard, and the effect was that of a ticking bomb.

Prop Ideas

Briefcase containing clock, wires, etc. (see above)

Prop gun

Documents (maps, passports, blueprints, etc.)

Camera

Related Dewey Subject List

Espionage (327.12)

Biographies of famous spies (*Agent Zigzag* by Ben Macintyre or *Fair Game* by Valerie Plame Wilson)

Notes

_____

_____

_____

_____

_____

_____

_____

_____

_____

_____

_____

_____

_____

_____

Booklist

Dale Brown. *Executive Intent*. William Morrow, 2010.
>   The world's superpowers are in a race to dominate not only the oceans but the Earth's orbit as well. Can Brown's hero Patrick McLanahan win the technological battle and prevent an all-out war?

Lee Child. *61 Hours*. Delacorte Press, 2010.
>   Jack Reacher is back in another countdown thriller. When a bus crash lands him in a small town in South Dakota, he meets the star witness in an upcoming drug trial. Unfortunately, a hired assassin would also like to meet this witness, and Jack has sixty-one hours to stop him.

Harlan Coben. *Play Dead*. Signet, 2010.
>   A reissue of an early Coben novel, this tells the story of a basketball star who dies on his honeymoon under mysterious circumstances and his beautiful wife's desperate investigation.

Michael Connelly. *The Fifth Witness*. Little, Brown and Company, 2011.
>   Lawyer Mickey Haller is back. When his client is accused of killing the banker about to foreclose on her house, Mickey knows he's on the right track when someone tries to kill him.

Robert Crais. *The Sentry*. G. P. Putnam's Sons, 2011.
>   When Joe Pike witnesses a gang trying to extort money from a local business, he offers his protection. Unfortunately, it will take both Pike and his friend Elvis Cole to figure out what other deadly threats might come true.

Clive Cussler. *The Jungle*. G. P. Putnam's Sons, 2011.
>   Part of Cussler's <u>Oregon Files</u> series, this installment finds Juan Cabrillo and his band of mercenaries trying to stop an ancient weapon that threatens world security.

Jonathan Kellerman. *Mystery*. Random House, 2011.
>   Another in Kellerman's series about crime-solving Los Angeles psychologist Alex Deleware. Along with homicide detective Milo Sturgis, Delaware races to discover the identity of a murdered woman who ate her last meal next to him the previous night.

T. Jefferson Parker. *Iron River*. Dutton, 2010.
>   An ATF agent who works the California-Mexico border vows to stop the "iron river," the flow of illegal arms that is fueling the drug cartels responsible for thousands of deaths.

James Patterson. *Toys*. Little, Brown and Company, 2011.
>   A pair of superhuman "Elites" are given the task of ending all human resistance to Elite control. But somehow one of them is torn from his perfect life and must now save all of humanity.

Ridley Pearson. *Killer Summer*. G. P. Putnam's Sons, 2009.
>   Idaho Sheriff Walt Fleming may be in trouble when a bomb goes off at a wine auction for the rich and famous held in his Sun Valley town. Who is responsible, and what else do they want?

History...Mystery

For those readers who like a little intrigue in their historical fiction, here is a display called "History . . . Mystery." It can be dressed up for a big wall display, or it can be as simple as a shelf display with just a booklist and a few titles in book holders. As with many other mystery subgenres, there are a lot of authors who write them, so filling out your inventory should be no problem. You might even be able to make a sub-subgenre: for example, historical mysteries set in ancient Rome or Medieval England.

For this display, there's a sample author list with the time period for their mysteries noted, as well as the featured detective.

Prop Ideas

Charcoal rubbing of hieroglyphics

Scrap of parchment

Broken shard of pottery

Prop skeleton parts

Related Dewey Subject List

Historical or narrative nonfiction (throughout 930–999)

Related Media

DVDs of History Channel programs

Notes

History Mystery Author List

Lindsey Davis
: Complex and rich in historical detail, this series is set in ancient Rome and features private investigator Marcus Didius Falco. Titles include *See Delphi and Die* (St. Martins, 2007).

Paul Doherty
: Often based on real incidents, these vivid mysteries feature Edward I's clerk and Keeper of the Secret Seal, Hugh Corbett. Titles include *The Waxman Murders* (Minotaur, 2010).

Michael Jecks
: Well-researched and multilayered mysteries set in Medieval England featuring Keeper of the Kings' Peace, Sir Baldwin Furnshill. Titles include *The King of Thieves* (Headline, 2008).

Sharan Newman
: Full of absorbing characters and well-developed plots, this series set in Medieval France features ex-novice nun Catherine Le Vendeur. Titles include *The Witch in the Well* (Forge, 2004).

Elizabeth Peters
: Beloved mysteries featuring Edwardian lady and amateur Egyptologist Amelia Peabody. Titles include *A River in the Sky* (William Morrow, 2010).

Laura Joh Rowland
: Detailed, political mysteries featuring Sano Ichiro, the Shogun's investigator, who solves crimes during the Genroku Period in Japan. Titles include *The Cloud Pavilion* (Minotaur, 2009).

Steven Saylor
: Gordianus the Finder is the investigator in this series full of period detail set in ancient Rome. Titles include *The Triumph of Caesar* (St. Martins Minotaur, 2008).

Victoria Thompson
: The cleverly plotted Gaslight mystery series features midwife Sarah Brandt who inhabits nineteenth-century New York. Titles include *Murder on Waverly Place* (Berkley Prime Crime, 2009).

Peter Tremayne
: Complex, political mystery series set in ancient Ireland featuring Celtic scholar Sister Fidelma and her companion Brother Eadulf. Titles include *The Dove of Death* (Minotaur, 2010).

Jacqueline Winspear
: Genteel mysteries featuring intrepid World War I–era London investigator Maisie Dobbs. Titles include *A Lesson in Secrets* (HarperCollins, 2011).

In the Good Old Summertime

If you've gotten tired of doing a "Beach Reads" book display year after year, try a different take on a summer display. This display is called "In the Good Old Summertime" and can be easily filled with books that simply have the word "summer" in the title. You can still use the same props that you use for the beach book display: sand pail and shovel, beach towel, sunglasses, and so on. But you end up with a wider variety of titles than just what people might read on vacation.

A friend of mine once did this display and put a lawn chair up on a table with books piled underneath and a photo of it ended up in the local newspaper. I wish I had that photo!

Prop Ideas

Beach towels

Beach toys

Sunglasses and sun screen

Water wings/life jacket

Lawn chair

Related Dewey Subject List

Barbecue cookbooks (641.57)

Picnic planning (641.578)

Baseball (796.357)

Summer/seasons (508.2)

Sandcastles (736.96)

Tide pools (577.699)

Notes

Booklist

Robin Antalek. *The Summer We Fell Apart.* Harper, 2009.

> Told from the point of view of four siblings who shared a chaotic childhood as the children of a struggling actress and a disillusioned playwright.

Lynn Kiele Bonasia. *Summer Shift.* Touchstone Books, 2010.

> As her great aunt struggles with Alzheimer's, Mary finds that she still harbors guilt over her husband's death a decade ago. Over the course of a summer, Mary finally begins to reconnect with those around her.

Robyn Carr. *A Summer in Sonoma.* Mira, 2010.

> The title says it all. Four friends spend a summer in Northern California trying to figure out their lives as they all prepare to celebrate their thirtieth birthdays.

Dorothea Benton Frank. *Lowcountry Summer.* William Morrow, 2010.

> Caroline's mother always presided over the family plantation, Tall Pines, with a queenly air. But after her mother's death, Caroline comes home and must face up to family responsibilities and truths.

Danielle Ganek. *The Summer We Read Gatsby.* Viking, 2010.

> Two estranged half-sisters inherit a Hamptons beach cottage known as "Fool's House" from their aunt. They arrive to find an artist in residence, a couple of old flames still burning, and a host of invitations to theme parties.

Agop J. Hacikyan. *A Summer without Dawn.* Interlink Books, 2010.

> Originally published in the early 1990s, this powerful story of the Armenian genocide in Turkey has been rereleased and is just as relevant as ever.

Heather Sharfeddin. *Windless Summer.* Delta Trade, 2009.

> Tom Jemmet owns a small hotel in the town of Rocket, located near the windsurfing paradise of the Columbia River Gorge. Unfortunately, there is no wind and no tourists, until a strange event in his hotel brings unwanted visitors and reveals long-hidden secrets.

Camilla Way. *The Dead of Summer.* Harcourt, 2007.

> Anita Naidu was the only survivor of a schoolyard murder. Now as an adult, she looks back on the crime and the surrounding events.

Susan Wiggs. *The Summer Hideaway.* Mira, 2010.

> Hospice nurse Claire Turner travels with her patient to a beautiful lakeside resort. Then his grandson, just back from Afghanistan, shows up and is suspicious of Claire's motives and her past.

Sherryl Woods. *Honeysuckle Summer.* Mira, 2010.

> Raylene escaped an abusive marriage and for over a year has been sheltered by her friends, the Sweet Magnolias. A story about family, friendship, and new love.

From *Ready-Made Book Displays* by Nancy M. Henkel. Santa Barbara, CA: Libraries Unlimited. Copyright © 2011.

Is There a Doctor in the House?

Since the early days of television, medical dramas have captivated audiences. Shows like *Marcus Welby MD, Emergency!, St. Elsewhere, ER, Grey's Anatomy, Scrubs, House,* and even *General Hospital* have all enjoyed substantial audiences. Undoubtedly, it is the life-and-death decisions being made, the smart and hunky actors heroically saving lives, and of course, the dramatic and romantic exploits of the characters.

Medical fiction has the same allure. In the hands of a talented writer, the reader can almost feel the pulse of the patient and hear the beep of the life-support system. Authors such as Robin Cook, Tess Gerritsen, and Michael Palmer are all staples in this category. You could also add some of the great nonfiction books published by and about doctors, hospitals, and illness, including *My Stroke of Insight* by Jill Bolte Taylor, *The House of Hope and Fear: Life in a Big City Hospital* by Audrey Young, and *Paradise General: Riding the Surge in a Combat Hospital in Iraq* by Dave Hnida.

Prop Ideas

Stethoscope

Medical bag

Scrubs

Photos of famous fictional physicians (Dr. Killdare, Dr. Quinn, Dr. McDreamy, etc. from Google images)

Related Dewey Subject List

Medical history (610.9)

Anatomy (611)

Hospitals (362.1109)

Notes

Booklist

Lauren Belfer. *A Fierce Radiance.* Harper, 2010.
>Part historical thriller, part romance, part pharmaceutical espionage. Claire Shipley is a reporter for *Life* in 1941 who is sent to cover a story about an experimental drug breakthrough: penicillin.

Ben Bova. *The Immortality Factor.* Tor, 2009.
>Stem cell research is a polarizing topic, and never more so than when it suddenly presents the opportunity for immortality and it puts two physician brothers on opposite sides of the argument.

Geraldine Brooks. *Year of Wonders.* Viking, 2001.
>In 1666, an English mountain village called Eyam, dubbed the "Plague Village" decides to quarantine itself to stop the spread of the disease. This is a test of faith and endurance that many villagers fail.

Candace Calvert. *Critical Care.* Tyndale House Publishers, 2009.
>A nurse-counselor and a hard-headed ER doctor disagree about the nurse's role in counseling trauma personnel. But faith and compromise might bring a meeting of the minds.

David Carnoy. *Knife Music.* Overlook Press, 2010.
>Emergency room surgeon Ted Cogan may be in big trouble. The teenage accident victim whose life he recently saved has committed suicide, and the police think he may be involved in her death.

Dianne Day. *Cut to the Heart: Clara Barton and the Darkness of Love and War.* Doubleday, 2002.
>This meticulously researched novel brings Red Cross founder and Civil War nurse Clara Barton to life, including the prejudice she faced and the private battles she fought.

Ken Follett. *The Third Twin.* Crown Publishers, 1996.
>A researcher stumbles onto a Cold War experiment involving genetics and twins. When she falls in love with one of a set of twins, she begins to worry if he shares traits with his criminal twin.

Frank Huyler. *Right of Thirst.* Harper Perennial, 2009.
>After his wife's death, cardiologist Charles Anderson goes to an Islamic country to help with earthquake relief, in hopes of forgetting his own troubles.

C. J. Lyons. *Lifelines.* Berkley Publishing Group, 2008.
>On her first day at Pittsburgh's Angels of Mercy Medical Center, attending physician Lydia Fiore loses a patient under suspicious circumstances. With the help of a few other women working at the hospital, she may figure out what is going on, and she just might hook up with that cute paramedic.

Robin Oliveira. *My Name Is Mary Sutter.* Viking, 2010.
>Young midwife Mary Sutter travels to Washington, D.C., during the Civil War to help tend the wounded. Ignoring pressure to return home, she ends up as the assistant to a well-known physician.

It's Academic

School has always been a popular subject for fiction authors. What kid hasn't read *Sideways Stories from Wayside School* or *Miss Bindergarten Gets Ready for Kindergarten*?

This is a great display to do in September at the start of the school year. Notice that almost all of the retailers in your town probably do the same thing: they capitalize on the fact that everyone is thinking about school and create elaborate displays to get people to buy new shoes, backpacks, and jeans for their kids.

This display could also work other times of year if you live in a college town. In my area, there are some regional college sports rivalries, so the week before a game I sometimes put up this display and include some mascot photos to draw patron attention.

Prop Ideas

Mortar board

Local college sweatshirt

Chalkboard

Apple

Pencils/notepad

Pom-poms

Related Dewey Subject List

GRE study guides (378.166)

College profile guides (378.73)

Scholarship/financial aid books (378.3)

Notes

_____

_____

_____

_____

_____

_____

_____

_____

_____

_____

_____

_____

_____

_____

Booklist

Kathleen Bacus. *Calamity Jayne Goes to College.* Love Spell, 2007.

    Tressa "Calamity" Jayne Turner is tired of blonde jokes, so she heads back to college (for the fourth time) determined to finally earn her degree and get a raise at the *Grandville Gazette*. But as her nickname implies, calamity follows her everywhere.

Elizabeth Bevarly. *Overnight Male.* HQN, 2008.

    Lila decides to leave her spy gig and agrees to one final mission in which she must go undercover as a university coed to catch a rogue agent. She may even end up undercover with her handsome new partner.

Willa Cather. *The Professor's House.* Vintage Books Classics Editions, 1990.

    Published in 1925, this is about a college professor who has become disillusioned, relates the life story of one of his students who was killed in World War I, and then ponders how to go on with this own life.

Susan Coll. *Acceptance.* Farrar, Straus & Giroux, 2007.

    Three seniors from Verona High head to a tiny liberal arts college that mistakenly got on a "Best Campus" list. This satirical look at the college selection and admission process will make you laugh and cringe.

Joanne Dobson. *Death without Tenure.* Poisoned Pen Press, 2010.

    An English professor competing for a tenure spot is the prime suspect when her main rival for the job is found dead.

Jean Hanff Korelitz. *Admission.* Grand Central Publishing, 2009.

    A Princeton University admissions officer is in the midst of deciding which of the many applications the school will accept when a secret from her past leads her to consider whether to make an admission of her own.

Ralph McInerny. *The Green Revolution.* Minotaur, 2008.

    One in a series about Notre Dame University professor Roger Knight and his brother Philip, a private investigator. When Roger suggests that Notre Dame refocus on academics when the football team isn't winning, he risks becoming a marked man.

Terry Pratchett. *Unseen Academicals.* HarperCollins, 2009.

    The very unathletic wizards of Unseen University must win a football match in which they are not allowed to use their magic. Part of Pratchett's <u>Discworld</u> novels.

Emily Raboteau. *The Professor's Daughter.* Henry Holt and Company, 2005.

    Emma's father is an Ivy League professor who has always kept his family at a distance. When her brother dies after a tragic accident, her family's past is revealed, and she faces her future.

Joanne Rendell. *The Professors' Wives' Club.* NAL Accent, 2008.

    A group of faculty wives at a Manhattan college meet and unite when the dean plans to bulldoze the common garden.

It's All Relative

The old maxim that you can choose your friends but you can't choose your family has fueled many fiction titles over the years. Stories about family dynamics and relationships elicit a gamut of feelings from readers: love, joy, anger, indulgence, jealousy, delight, indignation, and even hatred. In the hands of a talented writer, a story about family can make readers feel as though they are part of that family, for better or for worse.

When you do this display, start with books that have the name of a relative in the title. Try a catalog search crossing "fiction" with any word that names a member of a family: daughter, grandfather, niece, uncle, and so on. You might also include titles from authors who write epic family sagas, such as Barbara Taylor Bradford, John Jakes, Belva Plain, and Edward Rutherford, or books by authors adept at stories about familial love or angst.

Prop Ideas

Family tree template

Old family photos

Related Dewey Subject List

Genealogy (929.1028)

Birth order (155.924)

Baby names (929.44)

Heraldry (929.6)

Sibling rivalry (155.443 and 306.875)

Parenting (649)

Family reunion planning (394.2 and 793.2)

Related Media

CD-ROMs of genealogy software such as Family Tree Maker

Notes

_____

_____

_____

_____

_____

_____

_____

_____

_____

_____

_____

Booklist

Jenna Blum. *The Stormchasers*. Dutton, 2010.

Karena's dangerously bipolar brother, Charles, is obsessed with storms. When he escapes from a psychiatric hospital, she joins a storm-chaser group in a desperate attempt to track him down.

Carole Cadwalladr. *The Family Tree*. Dutton, 2005.

Rebecca Monroe's pregnancy prompts an interest in her family history, and the narrative explores several generations of her family and how they relate to her and to her unborn child.

Mary Carter. *My Sister's Voice*. Kensington Books, 2010.

Deaf artist Lacey Gears lives a successful life in Philadelphia. One day she receives a mysterious letter informing her that she has a twin sister, and suddenly nothing is as it seems.

Julian Cole. *The Amateur Historian*. Minotaur Books, 2010.

Sam Rounder is a chief inspector. His estranged brother, Rick, is now a local private investigator. Together they race to find a missing girl whose disappearance is linked to a century-old death.

Paul Doiron. *The Poacher's Son*. Minotaur Books, 2010.

Maine Game Warden Mike Bowditch finds out his father, a renowned local poacher and drinker, is a fugitive in a murder investigation.

Shilpi Somaya Gowda. *Secret Daughter*. William Morrow, 2010.

A baby girl from a Mumbai orphanage binds together both her birth family and the American couple that adopts her.

Kathleen Kent. *The Heretic's Daughter*. Little, Brown and Company, 2008.

Based on the author's family history, this is the story of one of many families torn apart by the hysteria of the Salem witch trials.

Lily King. *Father of the Rain*. Atlantic Monthly Press, 2010.

When Daley's parents divorce, she learns to navigate the vastly different households her parents have created. Then as an adult, she must decide whether to put her life on hold to save her father.

Amy Tan. *The Bonesetter's Daughter*. G. P. Putnam's Sons, 2001.

Tan, a master of mother-daughter stories, delivers a tale about a modern woman whose troubles begin to mirror her mother's life in a remote village in China.

Rob Thurman. *Chimera*. Roc, 2010.

After ten years, Stefan Korsak has finally found his kidnapped brother, Lukas, who, as part of an experiment, has been genetically altered into an assassin.

Just for Laughs

If beauty is in the eye of the beholder, humor is in the funny bone of the reader. Or something like that.

In no other area of readers' advisory do librarians have so much trouble matching books to readers, simply because what is hilarious to one person may be incomprehensible to someone else. For example, one reader may think Christopher Moore's books are a scream, and another reader might find them irreverent. One reader might chuckle at Carl Hiaasen's stories, while another might think they are offensive.

When you gather your inventory for this display, remember to include all kinds of humor in it, from the gentle down-home humor of writers like Fannie Flagg to the in-your-face absurdity of authors such as Tim Dorsey. You might also include some books by humor essayists such as Dave Barry, David Sedaris, and Sarah Vowell. Put this display up in April to coincide with National Humor Month.

Prop Ideas

Funny nose glasses

Rubber chicken

Whoopie cushion

Related Dewey Subject List

Joke books (398.6)

Humorous essays (814.54)

Circus clowns (791.33)

Stand-up comedy (792.7)

Notes

_____

_____

_____

_____

_____

_____

_____

_____

_____

_____

_____

_____

_____

_____

_____

_____

_____

Booklist

Meg Cabot. *Queen of Babble*. William Morrow, 2006.

>An American girl in London meets up with her unfaithful boyfriend at a wedding she is supposed to be bartending and, as usual, can't keep her mouth shut. First in a series.

Toni McGee Causey. *Bobbie Faye's (Kinda, Sorta, Not Exactly) Family Jewels*. St. Martin's Griffin, 2008.

>Spunky Bobbie Faye seems to attract disaster. When cousin Francesca needs help finding her dad's diamonds (stolen by her mother), Bobbie goes on the run and head-to-head with a sexy undercover agent.

Claire Cook. *Seven Year Switch*. Voice, 2010.

>Jill's husband, Seth, returns after departing suddenly for a seven-year stint in the Peace Corps. What's a girl to do? Go on vacation in Costa Rica, of course…

Lisa Lutz. *The Spellman Files*. Simon and Schuster, 2007.

>The first in a series of books about a hilariously dysfunctional family that owns a private investigation firm.

Evan Mandery. *First Contact, or, It's Later than You Think*. HarperCollins, 2010.

>A Douglas Adams–style satire about aliens from the planet Rigel-Rigel who arrive on Earth and urge us to shape up or be destroyed. But on the bright side, they really like our Bundt cakes.

Alexander McCall Smith. *The Unbearable Lightness of Scones*. Anchor Books, 2010.

>The inhabitants of 44 Scotland Street, an apartment house in Edinburgh, are back with their beloved foibles intact.

Rick Moody. *The Four Fingers of Death*. Little, Brown and Company, 2010.

>In 2025, a down-and-out author writes the novelization of a movie about a Martian-infected astronaut arm that attacks Earth, with one of its fingers missing.

Misa Ramirez. *Hasta la Vista, Lola!* Minotaur Books, 2010.

>Lola Cruz is a kung-fu-fighting, salsa-dancing private detective whose identity was stolen by a woman who promptly got killed. This follow-up to *Living la Vida Lola* is a funny, sexy romp.

Robert Rankin. *Hollow Chocolate Bunnies of the Apocalypse*. Gollancz, 2003.

>Someone is murdering nursery rhyme characters! When Jack comes to Toy City to make his fortune, he teams up with a teddy bear detective named Eddie to solve the crimes.

Ann B. Ross. *Miss Julia Meets Her Match*. Viking, 2004.

>An irrepressible and proper southern widow, Miss Julia must make an important decision when her longtime beau finally proposes. One in a series.

Let's Dance

Once upon a time, *American Bandstand* was one of the most popular shows on TV. Basically, it was just some musical guests and then some teenagers dancing. Since then, there have been both movies and TV shows dedicated to the dance world.

But it has been recent television shows such as *Dancing with the Stars* and *So You Think You Can Dance* that have really gotten people interested in learning to dance again. This display is a good way to capitalize on that interest.

Start with some dance fiction and then choose some books that help people learn various dances, or even some biographies of famous dancers and choreographers such as Maria Tallchief and George Balanchine. You may be surprised by the quantity and variety of dance fiction titles, such as the dance mysteries by Natalie M. Roberts with cute titles like *Pointe and Shoot* and *Tutu Deadly* as well as the many stand-alone titles on various types of dance.

Put this display up when your favorite dance show starts a new season or at the end of April to celebrate National Dance Week.

Prop Ideas

Dancing shoes (e.g., ballet or tap)

Top hat

Handheld musical instruments (castanets, tambourine, maracas, etc.)

Mirrored "disco" ball

Related Dewey Subject List

Learn to dance books (792.8 and 793.33)

Dance photography (779.97 and 792.8)

Biographies of famous dancers (e.g., Fred Astaire)

Related Media

DVDs of dance instruction or dance competitions

Notes

Booklist

Sarah Bird. *The Flamenco Academy.* Knopf, 2006.
> At a loss after personal tragedy, Rae and her friend Didi enroll in a flamenco class at the local university. Soon they are both obsessed with a flamenco guitarist, and the three become stars of the dance.

Carole Nelson Douglas. *Cat in a Topaz Tango.* Forge, 2009.
> A killer is stalking a Las Vegas celebrity dance festival. It's up to feline sidekick Midnight Louis to keep his human from waltzing into disaster.

Heather Graham. *Dead on the Dance Floor.* Mira, 2004.
> Quinn O'Casey goes undercover at a dance studio to investigate the death of the favored winner of the Universe of Champions dance competition.

Reyna Grande. *Dancing with Butterflies.* Washington Square Press, 2009.
> Four women of Mexican descent are united by their love of Folklorico dance.

Lloyd Jones. *Here at the End of the World We Learn to Dance.* Dial Press Trade Paperbacks, 2008.
> Parallel love stories across time are linked by the couples' love for each other and for the tango.

Keith Maillard. *The Clarinet Polka.* Thomas Dunne Books, 2003.
> When Jimmy Koprowski returns home from Vietnam to his Polish-American neighborhood, his healing is greatly helped when his sister starts an all-girl polka band.

Sharon Owens. *The Ballroom on Magnolia Street.* G. P. Putnam's Sons, 2004.
> The patrons of Johnny "Hollywood" Hogan's ballroom in Belfast are all looking for something: family, friendship, and even love.

Jocelyn Saint James. *One, Two, Three . . . Together.* Avalon Books, 2010.
> Liz needs a partner for a dance contest that could save her mother's dance studio. Tyler needs to get married to receive the trust fund that will save his fishing charter business. Sounds like a dance of convenience.

Kathryn Wagner. *Dancing for Degas.* Bantam Books, 2010.
> Alexandrie joins the Paris Opera ballet in hopes of supporting her peasant family. She becomes witness to the politics of the ballet world and falls in love with the painter who chronicles it, Edgar Degas.

Elizabeth White. *Tour de Force.* Zondervan, 2009.
> An inspirational romance about a talented ballet dancer and a dance company director who must decide if they are following God's plan or their own.

Louis L'Amour and More

The western genre has its loyal readers, and many of them have read the entire canon of Louis L'Amour's work. And although L'Amour is certainly king of the traditional western novel, along with Zane Grey, there are many other authors who write them as well. For this display, there is an author list with a sample title included.

To create a western display, you usually need only a few basic props to create the mood. Cowboy attire like a hat, boots, and a bandana always work well, as do pieces of cowboy equipment like a rope or a saddle blanket. Be careful that you don't violate the second law of book display: It's not about the props. It's easy to get so carried away with the cowboy theme that you forget that the purpose of the display is to showcase the books.

Prop Ideas

Rope

Cactus

Cowboy hat

Cowboy boots

Burlap (as drop cloth)

Bandana

Toy horses

Related Dewey Subject List

Old West history (978s)

Cowboys (978s)

Horses (636.1)

Biographies of Old West personalities (Wyatt Earp, Doc Holiday, Geronimo, etc.)

Ghost towns of the Old West (917.8)

Notes

Traditional Western Author List

Max Brand
Called one of the most celebrated western authors of all time, Brand is known for his dozens of short epic novels about men in the west. Titles include *Acres of Unrest* (Leisure, 2009).

Ralph Compton
Taut descriptions and a great supporting cast characterize Compton's novels, now written by Marcus Galloway, Joseph A. West, and others. Titles include *Death of a Hangman* (Signet, 2010).

Ralph Cotton
Once nominated for a Pulitzer Prize, Cotton's work is classic adventure set in the Old West. Titles include *Gun Country* (Signet, 2010).

Will Henry
Prolific author Will Henry won the Spur Award five times, as well as a lifetime achievement award for Western literature. Titles include *A Bullet for Billy the Kid* (Leisure, 2009).

William W. Johnstone
With an emphasis on great storytelling, Johnstone's books are full of real characters with real problems. Now being written by J. A. Johnstone. Titles include *Snake River Slaughter* (Pinnacle, 2010).

Elmer Kelton
Multiple Spur Award winner, Kelton books focus on real cowboys rather than mythic ones. Titles include *The Raiders: Sons of Texas* (Forge, 2006).

William Colt MacDonald
A prolific author of western books and western screenplays, MacDonald's book titles include *Powder Smoke* (Leisure, 2006).

Lauran Paine
Cowboy-turned-author Paine wrote westerns under his own name and many pseudonyms as well. Titles include *Feud on the Mesa* (Leisure, 2008).

Jory Sherman
A poet, a painter, and a prolific author of entertaining westerns filled with interwoven plots and characters. Titles include *Sidewinder* (Berkely Books, 2009).

Richard S. Wheeler
Prolific author best known for his western novels about trapper and guide Barnaby Skye. Titles include *The Owl Hunt* (Forge, 2010.)

From *Ready-Made Book Displays* by Nancy M. Henkel. Santa Barbara, CA: Libraries Unlimited. Copyright © 2011.

Love and Danger

If you are tired of doing displays of relationship books for Valentine's Day, change it up and do romantic suspense instead. There are tons of authors who write romantic suspense and many traditional romance authors who've jumped on this popular bandwagon. In fact, there are so many, I've included an author list with a sample title included. Chances are, if your patrons discover that they enjoy this genre, they'll be happy to have a list of other authors who write in the same vein.

Prop Ideas

Shadow outline of a man and woman, probably running and looking back over their shoulders

Paper hearts

Prop gun

Leather jacket

Pumps with stiletto heels

Lightning bolt image

Related Dewey Subject List

Dating/courtship (646.77)

Man-woman relationships (306.7)

Notes

_____

_____

_____

_____

_____

_____

_____

_____

_____

_____

_____

_____

_____

_____

_____

Romantic Suspense Author List

Beverly Barton

Award-winning author Barton's romantic suspense novels feature frightening murder scenes as well as happy endings. Titles include *Worth Dying For* (HQN, 2010).

Suzanne Brockmann

Featuring smart women and hunky ex-Navy SEALs, titles include *Breaking the Rules* (Ballantine, 2011) and often focus on the Troubleshooter, Inc. operatives.

Barbara Freethy

Freethy mixes suspense, romance, and heart in her stories and characters. Titles include *Silent Run* (ONYX, 2008).

Cindy Gerard

Gerard's sexy suspense novels include two series, one featuring bodyguards and the other the men of Black Ops, Inc. Titles include *Whisper No Lies* (Pocket Star Books, 2009).

Tara Janzen

Fast-paced action and hot romance are the hallmark of Janzen's books. Titles include *Breaking Loose* (Dell Publishing, 2009).

Carla Neggers

Adventure, romance, suspense, and even humor abound in this prolific author's stories. Titles include *The Whisper* (Mira, 2010).

Karen Robards

Robards writes books with great characters, spicy romance, and a dash of humor. Titles include *Shattered* (G. P. Putnam's Sons, 2010).

J. D. Robb

The pseudonym of Nora Roberts, J. D. Robb writes the futuristic <u>In Death</u> series about New York police officer Eve Dallas and her husband, Roarke. Titles include *Indulgence in Death* (G. P. Putnam's Sons, 2010).

Christina Skye

Skye's books feature romance, intrigue, and even some paranormal activity. Titles include *To Catch a Thief* (HQN, 2008).

Anne Stuart

Award-winning novelist Anne Stuart has written in several romance genres, including her romantic suspense <u>Ice</u> series. Titles include *Fire and Ice* (Mira, 2008).

Much Ado about the Bard

This is a fun display to do because although many people are turned off by the idea of reading a Shakespeare play, they are often intrigued enough to read a novel about him or one of his plays. Put this display up in April to commemorate his birthday on the 23rd, or to coincide with the release of a movie version of one of the plays.

This display lends itself well to a display case or to a big wall display, and it looks nice when you give it the illusion of being on a stage. If you have a nice piece of velvet or brocade, use a wooden dowel to fashion a curtain to create the proscenium arch effect.

The booklist included for this display is really just the tip of the iceberg. There are many authors who have written works of fiction about Shakespeare or have reimagined his plays. See what you've got on the shelves at your library.

Prop Ideas

Curtain draped over a dowel

Various Shakespeare portraits (available on Google images)

Tragedy/comedy masks (real masks or images of them)

"Which Shakespeare Play?" Quiz (see page 106)

Playbills from Shakespearean plays

Names of the plays printed on cardstock

Related Dewey Subject List

Shakespeare biographies (928 or Biography section)

Biographies of famous Shakespearean actors (927 or Biography section)

History of the Globe Theater (792s)

Shakespeare's plays (822.33)

Shakespeare's sonnets (821.3)

Books about film versions of the plays (791.4372)

Film versions of the plays (DVD fiction and DVD 822.33)

Graphic novel editions of plays (822.33)

Related Media

DVDs of stage or film adaptations of Shakespeare's plays

Notes

_____

_____

_____

_____

_____

_____

_____

Booklist

Elizabeth Bear. *Ink and Steel: A Novel of the Promethean Age.* Roc, 2008.
> Will Shakespeare and Kit Marley team up to stop factions of the Faerie realm that aim to destroy England.

Jennifer Lee Carrell. *Haunt Me Still.* Dutton, 2010.
> During a production of the "Scottish play," directors Kate and Ben discover there just might be something to the curse of *Macbeth* after all.

Anne Fortier. *Juliet.* Ballantine Books, 2010.
> After her aunt's death, Julie is given a key to a safe deposit box in Italy, which leads to a centuries-old family feud. Will she discover who she really is, and, more important, will she find her Romeo?

Philip Gooden. *Mask of Night: A Shakespearean Murder Mystery.* Carroll and Graf, 2004.
> One of several murder mysteries featuring actor and sleuth Nick Revill.

Lori Handeland. *Shakespeare Undead.* St. Martin's Griffin, 2010.
> Jane Austen and zombies? It's been done. Now it's Shakespeare's turn.

Simon Hawke. *Much Ado about Murder.* Forge, 2002.
> One of several Elizabethan theater mysteries featuring Shakespeare and co-thespian Symington Smythe.

Faye Kellerman. *The Quality of Mercy.* Avon Books, 2002.
> Rebecca, a beautiful young woman close to Elizabeth's court, dresses like a man to experience adventure, with Will Shakespeare as her guide.

Christopher Rush. *Will.* Overlook Press, 2008.
> The richly told story of Shakespeare on his deathbed as he dictates his will and comes to terms with his life.

Jess Winfield. *My Name Is Will: A Novel of Sex, Drugs, and Shakespeare.* Twelve, 2008.
> This irreverent romp is the parallel story of grad student Willie Shakespeare Greenberg and budding playwright William Shakespeare as they each try to find their way in the world.

Which Shakespeare Play?

Name the Shakespeare play that contains each famous line below.

_____ 1. To be or not to be,--that is the question.

_____ 2. Et tu, Brute?

_____ 3. All the world's a stage and all the men and women merely players.

_____ 4. Then must you speak of one who lov'd not wisely but too well.

_____ 5. Good night! Good night! Parting is such sweet sorrow.

_____ 6. A horse! A horse! My kingdom for a horse!

_____ 7. What a piece of work is man.

_____ 8. Friends, Romans, countrymen, lend me your ears!

_____ 9. We are such stuff as dreams are made on.

_____ 10. Beware the ides of March.

_____ 11. The green-eyed monster.

_____ 12. Why, then the world's mine oyster.

_____ 13. If music be the food of love, play on!

_____ 14. The lady doth protest too much, methinks.

_____ 15. All that glisters is not gold.

_____ 16. Nothing can come of nothing.

_____ 17. Though this be madness, yet there is method in't.

_____ 18. Eye of newt, and toe of frog.

_____ 19. Off with his head!

_____ 20. The course of true love never did run smooth.

Answers: 1. Hamlet 2. Julius Caesar 3. As You Like It 4. Othello 5. Romeo & Juliet 6. Richard III 7. Hamlet 8. Julius Caesar 9. The Tempest 10. Julius Caesar 11. Othello 12. The Merry Wives of Windsor 13. Twelfth Night 14. Hamlet 15. The Merchant of Venice 16. King Lear 17. Hamlet 18. Macbeth 19. Richard III 20. A Midsummer Night's Dream

Outside of a Dog

Groucho Marx said it best: "Outside of a dog, a book is man's best friend. Inside of a dog, it's too dark to read." This little quote has been the basis of a perennially popular dog fiction display at my library. It works as a tabletop display with a big dog bed full of books and a giant dog dish full of kibble, and it works as a more simple point-of-checkout display with just a couple of stuffed dogs.

Along with the dog fiction, you could include dog training and dog breed books, as well as lovable dog nonfiction such as *Marley and Me* by John Grogan or classics like *Call of the Wild* by Jack London. Put this display up in February in honor of the annual Westminster Kennel Club Dog Show or in October for the American Humane Association's Adopt-a-Dog Month.

Prop Ideas

Leash

Dog dish

Dog collar

Dog biscuits

Related Dewey Subject List

Dog breeds (636.71)

Dog/puppy training (636.708)

Service dogs (362.4048)

Dog tricks (636.72)

Notes

_____

_____

_____

_____

_____

_____

_____

_____

_____

_____

_____

_____

_____

_____

_____

Booklist

Laurien Berenson. *Doggie Day Care Murder.* Kensington, 2008.

    Melanie Travis: dog lover, amateur sleuth. This time around, Melanie is checking out a day-care center for dogs when she discovers the corpse of the owner.

Pierre Davis. *A Breed Apart.* Bantam Dell, 2009.

    It's a change of pace from most medical thrillers when the patient is a dog. In this case, a research dog with a super-brain is kidnapped in an attempt to save a wealthy eccentric.

Mark Haddon. *The Curious Incident of the Dog in the Night-Time.* Doubleday, 2003.

    Not about a dog exactly, but about the death of a dog and an autistic teen determined to track down its killer.

Eva Hornung. *Dog Boy.* Viking, 2010.

    A harsh story set in a harsh place. When four-year-old Romochka is abandoned in Moscow by his mother, he is taken in by a pack of feral dogs.

Karin Lowachee. *The Gaslight Dogs.* Orbit, 2010.

    A spirit walker from an Arctic tribe must teach an officer from a southern tribe to harness the talent they share—the ability to form a physical manifestation of their spirits into the shape of The Dog.

Judi McCoy. *Death in Show.* Obsidian, 2010.

    With the help of her boyfriend, Detective Sam Ryder, professional dog walker Ellie Engelman is determined to solve the mystery of the dog show killer.

Spencer Quinn. *Dog on It.* Atria Books, 2009.

    The first of the Chet and Bernie mysteries series featuring Chet, the K-9 school dropout who narrates the books, and his private investigator Bernie, who understands all of Chet's doggie methods of communication.

David Rosenfelt. *Dog Tags.* Grand Central Publishing, 2010.

    Andy Carpenter is a wise-cracking, dog-loving defense attorney. This time around, his client is an ex-police dog and his owner, an Iraqi war vet, who are wrongly accused of murder.

Kandy Shepherd. *Love Is a Four-Legged Word.* Berkely Sensation, 2009.

    Brutus is spoiled and cranky, and he has just inherited a multimillion dollar estate. Tom is his lawyer. Madeline is his guardian. Did I mention that Brutus is a dog?

Garth Stein. *The Art of Racing in the Rain.* HarperCollins, 2008.

    Denny Swift is a race car driver whose wife dies tragically, leaving him in a custody battle with his in-laws. Denny's story is told by Enzo, his dog.

Passages from India

I like doing displays based on fiction set in other countries because it is easy to do a catalog search and find numerous titles. When I do a display based on Indian fiction, I usually do a mix between historical fiction and modern India as well as throwing in classics such as E. M. Forster's *A Passage to India*, M. M. Kaye's *The Far Pavilions*, Hermann Hesse's *Siddhartha*, and Kamala Markandaya's *Nectar in a Sieve*.

Decorating this display can be as simple as using Google Image photos of the Taj Mahal or Bollywood stars, or you could use colorful fabric swatches to liven it up. For my display, I use a bed spread that my brother-in-law bought for me in Mumbai.

Prop Ideas

Cloth with Indian print/motif

Taj Mahal photos

Map of India

Related Dewey Subject List

History of India (954)

Travel in India (915.4)

Indian cooking (641.5954)

Related Media

DVDs on travel to India or Indian cooking

Notes

_____

_____

_____

_____

_____

_____

_____

_____

_____

_____

_____

_____

_____

_____

Booklist

Anne Cherian. *A Good Indian Wife*. W. W. Norton, 2008.

    Neel Sarath enjoys the bachelor life as an anesthesiologist in San Francisco. When his family lures him home to India for an arranged marriage, he finds his bride is not quite what he expected.

Kiran Desai. *The Inheritance of Loss*. Atlantic Monthly Press, 2006.

    A bitter old man lives at the foot of the Himalayas. His quiet life is interrupted by Indian-Nepali insurgents and the arrival of his orphaned teenage granddaughter.

Chitra Banerjee Divakaruni. *The Palace of Illusions*. Doubleday, 2008.

    The Mahabharat, an ancient Indian epic, is retold from the point of view of Panchaali, a woman married to five mythological brothers trying to reclaim their inheritance.

Advaita Kala. *Almost Single*. Bantam Discovery, 2009.

    Aisha is a modern single girl in New Delhi, a city with old traditions that say it is long overdue for her to be married. Her mother says the same thing.

Bharati Mukherjee. *Desirable Daughters*. Theia, 2002.

    Three sisters born in Calcutta live very different lives on two continents until danger brings them back together.

Anita Nair. *Ladies Coupe*. St. Martin's Griffin, 2004.

    Six women traveling to a seaside resort in a "ladies only" train car meet and share their stories.

Indu Sundaresan. *The Twentieth Wife*. Washington Square Press, 2002.

    The first volume in the <u>Taj Mahal Trilogy</u> introduces Mehrunnisa, whose role as Prince Salim's wife helps shape the destiny of the Mughal empire.

Manil Suri. *The Age of Shiva*. W. W. Norton, 2008.

    Hindu myth and modern India meet in a story set just after the Indian independence from Britain.

Vikas Swarup. *Q and A: A Novel*. Scribner, 2005.

    A young man from the Mumbai slums wins a billion rupees on a television game show and brings himself unwanted attention. Made into a film titled *Slumdog Millionnaire*.

Padma Viswanathan. *The Toss of a Lemon*. Harcourt, 2008.

    Based on the author's family history, this is the story of the caste system in India and how it affects three generations of a family and one child bride.

Put Your Best Foot Forward

Here's yet another display that happened because I suddenly had a handful of books in front of me with cover art that was eerily similar. This time it was feet. Shoes, feet, toes, and lower legs are a popular cover image, as are ladies' backs (see "Back in Circulation" display).

Whenever I do this display, my coworkers always want to contribute their footwear, and I often ask for specific shoes to round out the display. For example, one woman has a tiny shoe made for a Chinese girl with a bound foot. Another coworker has a beautiful set of beaded moccasins from the Shoshone tribe. Someone else loans me her bright red cowboy boots, and still someone else has a set of Italian military shoes complete with spats. We all put our best feet forward for this display.

Prop Ideas

Footprints

Shoes

Shoe boxes

Shoe horn

Socks

Pedicure kit

Related Dewey Subject List

History of shoes (391.413)

Footwear industry (338.768)

Foot care (617.585)

Notes

Booklist

Sherman Alexie. *War Dances.* Grove Press, 2009.
> A collection of short stories and poems united by a common theme of men in transition.

Rebecca Boschee. *Mulligan Girl.* Avalon Books, 2010.
> A sweet romance about a secret shopper who pretends to be married while checking out a golf course. She meets the man of her dreams, but he thinks she's unavailable.

Jennifer Crusie. *Bet Me.* St. Martin's Press, 2004.
> A fun, modern love story about a handsome guy who won't commit and a girl who wears great shoes and doesn't believe in true love. Fate wants to prove them both wrong.

Sheila Curran. *Everyone She Loved.* Atria Books, 2009.
> Penelope has love, friends, family, and money. Then she dies, and her will stipulates that her husband can only remarry with everyone's consent, creating a fragile bond among all those she loved.

Sijie Dai. *Balzac and the Little Chinese Seamstress.* Knopf, 2002.
> Two young men are sent to the Chinese countryside for "reeducation" during the Cultural Revolution and discover a stash of translated works of Western literature. Thus begins their real reeducation.

Dorothy Koomson. *My Best Friend's Girl.* Bantam Books, 2008.
> Kamryn's former best friend, Adele, betrayed her. Now, Adele is dying and asks Kamryn to adopt her daughter, who is at the center of the betrayal.

Alexander McCall Smith. *Blue Shoes and Happiness.* Pantheon Books, 2006.
> Part of the No. 1 Ladies' Detective Agency series, this time around Precious Ramotswe is investigating the local advice columnist.

Audrey Niffenegger. *The Time Traveler's Wife.* Harcourt, 2003.
> Henry is a charismatic librarian married to Clare, a beautiful artist. Can love conquer even Henry's Chrono-Displacement Disorder—a condition that makes him involuntarily travel through time?

Charles Webb. *Home School.* Thomas Dunne Books, 2008.
> The long-awaited sequel to Webb's classic novel *The Graduate* finds Ben and Elaine in conflict with the local school board when they educate their sons at home. Mrs. Robinson (now known as Nan) to the rescue.

Read a Variety of Fruits and Vegetables

Have you ever wondered what to do with all that plastic food that your kids had in their grocery store play set? Plastic bananas, cucumbers, apples, oranges and carrots are all part of the set my kids had. One day I was weeding in the stacks and saw a book with a photo of plastic food on the cover and thought, "There's an idea for the fake food my kids used to play with."

While searching for books for this display inventory, you may discover that there are more books with fruit in the title than vegetables, but don't let that stop you. Do a catalog search for as many kinds of produce as you can think of, put a bowl of plastic fruit next to it, and see what happens. Bon appétit.

Prop Ideas

Plastic fruit and vegetables in a bowl

Table setting

Related Dewey Subject List

Vegetarian cookbooks (641.5636)

Vegetable gardening (635)

Orchards (634.0973)

Nutrition (613.2)

Notes

_____

_____

_____

_____

_____

_____

_____

_____

_____

_____

_____

_____

_____

_____

_____

_____

_____

Booklist

Merlinda Bobis. *Banana Heart Summer.* Delta Trade Paperbacks, 2008.
>A coming-of-age story set one summer in the Philippines in which Nenita tries to overcome her family's poverty by becoming a housemaid for wealthy neighbors.

Mark Dunn. *Ella Minnow Pea: A Novel in Letters.* Anchor Books, 2002.
>The leaders on the island of Nollop have decided to progressively ban letters of the alphabet, making communication increasingly difficult. Can Ella save her family, friends, and the island folk?

Fannie Flagg. *Fried Green Tomatoes at the Whistle Stop Café.* Ballantine Books, 2000.
>The story of friends Idgie and Ruth who run a small café in Alabama in the 1930s.

Mohammed Hanif. *A Case of Exploding Mangoes.* Alfred A. Knopf, 2008.
>The dictator of Pakistan dies in a mysterious plane crash, and Ali Shigri's father commits suicide under equally suspicious circumstances. A mix of politics, the military, and magical realism.

Joanne Harris. *Five Quarters of the Orange.* Morrow, 2001.
>As a young girl, Franboise Simon lived in a tiny French village occupied by the Nazis during World War II. She returns home as a widow and finds that the past may be there waiting for her.

Julie Hyzy. *State of the Onion.* Berkely, 2008.
>One in a series about amateur sleuth Olivia Paras, who just happens to be the first woman chef at the White House.

Marian Keyes. *Watermelon.* Perennial, 2002.
>This was the debut novel by a popular author about a London woman whose husband leaves her the day their daughter is born and how it changes her life for the better.

Marina Lewycka. *Strawberry Fields.* Penguin Press, 2007.
>A group of migrant workers from a strawberry field in England embark on a cross-country journey after the strawberry farmer's wife tries to run him over with a sports car.

Nancy Pickard. *The Blue Corn Murders.* Delacorte Press, 1998.
>After the death of author Virginia Rich, Nancy Pickard was commissioned to take over authorship of Rich's Eugenia Potter series. This time around, Eugenia hopes to vacation at an archeological camp and instead gets murder and recipes.

L. J. Washburn. *A Peach of a Murder.* Signet, 2006.
>The first in the "fresh-baked" mystery series finds amateur sleuth Phyllis Newsom determined to win first prize in the Peach Festival pie-baking contest.

Read Through the Year

When I was a child, my favorite book was *The Wednesday Witch* by Ruth Chew. It was about a witch who rode on a canister vacuum instead of a broom and went around shrinking things down so she could put them in her pocket and take them back to her cave. Books with days of the week in the title obviously hold special meaning for me because of that odd witch.

To gather inventory for "Read Through the Year," do catalog searches for fiction crossed with the names of the days of the week, the months of the year, and even the seasons. An easy one is the series by Harry Kemelman about Rabbi David Small—the books have the days of the week in the title.

Prop Ideas

Calendar pages

Page-a-day calendar

Sundial

Related Dewey Subject List

History of the calendar (529.3)

Calendar folklore (394)

World history timelines (902)

Notes

_____

_____

_____

_____

_____

_____

_____

_____

_____

_____

_____

_____

_____

_____

_____

_____

_____

_____

_____

_____

Booklist

Tom Clancy. *The Hunt for Red October.* Berkley Books, 1985.
> The novel that introduced Jack Ryan to the world. Two subs, one American and one Soviet, are searching for a renegade Soviet submarine skippered by a commander hoping to defect to the United States.

Jasper Fforde. *Thursday Next: First among Sequels.* Viking, 2007.
> This time around Thursday Next, the literary detective, is trying to find the lost humor in Thomas Hardy novels and solve the death of Sherlock Holmes.

Julia Glass. *Three Junes.* Pantheon Books, 2002.
> Set years apart in three different Junes, this novel follows the Scottish McLeod family—their lives, deaths, friendships, and loves.

Kate Jacobs. *The Friday Night Knitting Club.* G. P. Putnam's Sons, 2007.
> Walker and Daughter is a little knit shop in Manhattan. Each week a group of friends gather to knit and share their lives.

Ian McEwan. *Saturday.* Nan A. Talese, 2005.
> A day in the life of London neurosurgeon Henry Perowne in which he plays squash, shops for dinner, and then thwarts an intruder at a family reunion.

James Patterson. *4th of July.* Little, Brown and Company, 2005.
> An installment of the prolific Patterson's Women's Murder Club finds club founder Lindsay Boxer facing a police brutality charge and a killer with a familiar motive.

Kris Radish. *The Sunday List of Dreams.* Bantam Books, 2007.
> Connie is recently retired and divorced. As she cleans up the detritus of her old life, she discovers a secret about her estranged daughter that puts her on a plane to New York City.

Kathy Reichs. *Monday Mourning.* Scribner, 2004.
> A mystery featuring popular forensic anthropologist Tempe Brennan in which she discovers some skeletons at a pizza restaurant.

Anita Shreve. *A Wedding in December.* Little, Brown and Company, 2005.
> A weekend wedding in the Berkshires brings together a group of high school friends, all of whom have secrets and are facing their own mortality.

Dalia Sofer. *The Septembers of Shiraz.* Ecco/HarperCollins, 2007.
> As the Ayatollah Khomeini's rule in Iran begins, a wealthy gem dealer in Tehran is falsely imprisoned, and his family struggles with the forces of class and politics as they attempt his release.

Reading Makes Cents

Most patrons appreciate a good play on words, and this is one that works pretty well. Use a display flyer with the title of the display and a back-drop photo showing piles of cash. Money always catches the eye, and patrons always double-take to look at the display.

The easiest way to fill this display is to do a keyword search crossing fiction and any words you can think of having to do with commerce: money, cash, dollar, coins, million, and so on. Examples of titles you will find include two Robert B. Parker novels: *Spare Change* featuring Sunny Randall and the <u>Spencer</u> novel *Hundred-Dollar Baby*. There is also *Firecracker* by Ray Shannon with a nice cover image of a $100 bill about to explode.

Put up this display to coincide with tax day on April 15 or on "Tax Free" day whenever that happens to fall. You could also put it up to highlight library programs on budgeting or financial planning.

Prop Ideas

Play money

Monopoly game board

Empty checkbooks/check registers

Related Dewey Subject List

Financial planning/budgeting (332.024)

Investing (332.6)

History of money (737.409)

Coin collecting (737.49)

Notes

Booklist

Loren Estleman. *The Left-Handed Dollar.* Forge, 2010.
>   Amos Walker, Estleman's hard-boiled Detroit detective, is hired to investigate an old crime perpetrated by "Joey Ballistic," a man well versed in the art of the "left-handed dollar."

Dick Francis. *Even Money.* G. P. Putnam's Sons, 2009.
>   The Royal Ascot, arguably the world's most famous horse-racing event, is the backdrop for this story of a bookmaker whose long-lost father appears and delivers a dire warning just as he dies from a stabbing by an unknown attacker.

Ed McBain. *Money, Money, Money.* Pocket Books, 2001.
>   It's Christmas time for the guys of McBain's 87th Precinct, but there are still bodies, including one that ends up in a trash can carrying a wad of cash and another that ends up half-eaten in the lion's cage at the zoo.

Joyce Meyer. *The Penny.* Faith Words, 2007.
>   When abused teenager Jenny Blake stops to pick up a penny, she inadvertently sets off a chain of events that brings her a healing relationship and faith that God has a plan for her life.

Arturo Perez-Reverte. *The King's Gold.* G. P. Putnam's Sons, 2008.
>   Swordsman-for-hire Captain Alatriste returns home to Spain short of cash until he is offered a dangerous job by the king himself.

Terry Pratchett. *Making Money.* HarperCollins, 2007.
>   Moist von Lipwig, Pratchett's <u>Discworld</u> hero, first introduced in *Going Postal*, is back and is now being asked to overhaul Ankh-Morpork's financial system.

Christopher Reich. *The First Billion.* Delacorte Press, 2002.
>   Former fighter pilot John "Jet" Gavallan, is now the CEO of a security company that gets involved with a Russian tech company that just happens to be run by the Russian mafia.

Roxana Robinson. *Cost.* Farrar, Straus & Giroux, 2008.
>   Art professor Julie Lambert goes to her family's Maine home for the summer and discovers that her mother is in the beginning stages of Alzheimer's and her younger son is addicted to heroin.

Sarah Strohmeyer. *The Penny Pinchers Club.* Dutton, 2009.
>   From the author who created the wacky Bubbles Yablonsky comes a story of a shopaholic who joins a support group to learn how to save money—and her marriage.

Stuart Woods. *Two Dollar Bill.* G. P. Putnam's Sons, 2005.
>   In this installment of the Stone Barrington novels, the New York lawyer takes on a client from Texas who happens to be a con man with a big stash of two dollar bills.

Riddle, Mystery, Enigma

When *The Da Vinci Code* first came out, there were thousands of holds on it, and we librarians were scrambling to find read-alikes for a book we hadn't been able to get hold of yet ourselves. Puzzles, secrets, and literary riddles are still a popular genre. Do a catalog search for fiction books with the word "secret" in the title, and you'll see what I mean. People are fascinated by enigmas and often enjoy reading about characters who examine and uncover the unexplained.

This is a display that works on a small scale as a shelf display or as a point-of-checkout display. You could also do this around Halloween instead of your usual display of ghost stories: create a display of fiction about unexplained mysteries, and combine it with some nonfiction about paranormal phenomenon or other unexplained, enigmatic topics.

Prop Ideas

Box wrapped in brown paper, covered in question marks

Puzzle pieces (regular or enlarged)

Related Dewey Subject List

Codes and ciphers (652.8)

Unexplained phenomena (001.94 and 031.02)

Puzzles (793.73)

Notes

_____

_____

_____

_____

_____

_____

_____

_____

_____

_____

_____

_____

_____

_____

_____

_____

_____

_____

_____

_____

Booklist

Terry Brennan. *The Sacred Cipher.* Kregel Publications, 2009.

> Mystery! History! Action! When an ancient scroll suddenly appears in New York, a group of historians and scientists race against time and unknown enemies to solve its secrets.

Geraldine Brooks. *People of the Book.* Viking, 2008.

> While in the process of preserving a rare Hebrew manuscript, Hanna Heath uncovers some intriguing artifacts hidden in the binding. These artifacts reveal much more than just the history of the manuscript.

Michael Cox. *The Glass of Time.* W. W. Norton and Company, 2008.

> A sequel to *The Meaning of Night*, this novel is set twenty years later and features a lady's maid (who is not a lady's maid at all) who is sent on "a great task" to uncover some lost secrets.

Umberto Eco. *The Name of the Rose.* Harcourt Brace, 1994.

> A literary, historical mystery set in 1327 in which coded symbols and manuscripts may hold the key to solving a series of murders.

Jane Langton. *The Escher Twist.* Viking, 2002.

> One is a series of mysteries featuring Homer and Mary Kelly. This time around, a woman disappears from an Escher exhibit being held at Cambridge, and the sleuths are pulled into an Escher-esque mystery. Book includes line drawings throughout.

Brad Meltzer. *The Book of Lies.* Grand Central, 2008.

> Superman, Cain and Abel, and an unsolved murder in the 1930s are all connected by a missing weapon and a mysterious organization known as "the Leadership."

Kate Mosse. *Labyrinth.* G. P. Putnam's Sons, 2006.

> Two women, Alice and Alais, born over eight centuries apart, are linked by a sacred book, a ring, and, of course, a labyrinth.

Matthew Pearl. *The Dante Club.* Random House, 2003.

> Members of the literary society, the Dante Club, are working to promote and translate *The Inferno*, but all is threatened by a series of murders that recreate scenes from the epic.

James Rollins. *The Doomsday Key.* William Morrow, 2009.

> In his inimitable style, Rollins brings back the Sigma team as its members face curses, codes, and ancient manuscripts in a thriller full of twists and turns.

Arturo Sangalli. *Pythagoras' Revenge: A Mathematical Mystery.* Princeton University Press, 2009.

> Two mathematicians on opposite sides of the Atlantic must work together to solve mathematical puzzles that may lead to a lost manuscript written by Pythagoras.

Royal Reads

I have a coworker who loves royal history. She knows the history of the British monarchy inside and out. She's read everything by Antonia Fraser and Alison Weir, and when she came up with the idea of a display called "All Things Tudor," I thought she might be on to something. I suggested we expand beyond the Tudors and do a display of fiction about European royalty. We did a catalog fiction search for books with any royal moniker in the title. Jean Plaidy, Robin Maxwell, and Philippa Gregory all had a wealth of potential books.

For the display we used a very regal looking velvet cloth and a crown I bought at the dollar store in a simulated crown jewels exhibit. The other small bits of princess-y jewelry came from my seven-year-old daughter's jewelry box. We put it on a table top for the best visibility, although it would probably work as a point-of-checkout display if you have enough counter space.

If you are strapped for books about royalty, you can always add a couple of classics such as Taylor Caldwell's *Captains and the Kings*, Pat Conroy's *The Prince of Tides*, and Robert Penn Warren's *All the King's Men*, even though they are about different types of royalty altogether.

Prop Ideas

Crown

Royal-looking costume jewelry

Purple cloth

Photo images of castles

Related Dewey Subject List

Biographies of famous kings or queens

British royalty (941.0099)

French royalty (944.033)

Related Media

DVDs of movies or television dramas about royalty (for example, *The Queen* starring Helen Mirren and *The Tudors* starring Jonathan Rhys-Meyers)

Notes

_____

_____

_____

_____

_____

_____

_____

_____

_____

_____

_____

_____

Booklist

Shana Abe. *Queen of Dragons*. Bantam Books, 2008.
> Part of Abe's series of romantic fantasies about the drakon, a race of beautiful shape-shifters who can change to either smoke or dragons. In this installment, the English drakon discover that they may not be the last tribe after all.

Rhys Bowen. *A Royal Pain*. Berkley Prime Crime, 2008.
> Lady Georgie is asked by the Queen to entertain a Bavarian princess and possibly even get the Prince of Wales to fall in love with her so he'll forget about that Mrs. Simpson. Unfortunately, the princess learned her English from gangster films and is an incurable shoplifter.

Fiona Buckley. *The Siren Queen*. Scribner, 2004.
> Ursula Blanchard is the illegitimate half-sister and lady-in-waiting to Queen Elizabeth I and sometimes her spy. This time around Buckley's heroine may have found a husband for her daughter, and she may also have uncovered a plot to put Mary, Queen of Scots on the throne.

Dorothy Dunnett. *The Game of Kings*. Vintage Books, 1997.
> The first in Dunnett's iconic <u>Lymond Chronicles</u>, in which Francis Crawford of Lymond returns to Scotland in 1547, despite the fact that he is wanted for treason.

Anne Easter Smith. *The King's Grace*. Simon & Schuster, 2009.
> Grace is the illegitimate daughter of Edward IV, as well as the half-sister of the two princes who disappeared in the Tower of London. When a young man claiming to be one of the princes arrives in court, the investigation that ensues may help Grace find her own place in the royal family.

C. W. Gortner. *The Last Queen*. Ballantine Books, 2008.
> Juana of Castile, daughter of Spanish rulers Isabel and Ferdinand, thinks she'll lead a happy life when she is married off to the Archduke of Flanders. When she unexpectedly inherits the throne of Spain, she is thrown into a power struggle against not only her husband, but all the rulers of Europe.

Mark Helprin. *Freddy and Fredericka*. Penguin Press, 2005.
> After one too many blunders, Freddy and Fredericka, who also happen to be the Prince and Princess of Wales, are sent packing to America to conquer the barbarian land. Instead, they ride the rails, fight forest fires, impersonate medical professionals, and work on a presidential campaign.

Camilla Lackberg. *The Ice Princess*. Pegasus Books, 2009.
> When writer Erica Falck returns home from Stockholm, she discovers the body of an old friend. When her friend's parents ask Erica to write about her, she begins to uncover secrets that many in the tiny Swedish coastal village might wish to remain hidden.

Susan Holloway Scott. *The Countess and the King*. New American Library, 2010.
> Katherine Sedley eschews a respectable marriage to become mistress of the married Duke of York. When he suddenly becomes King James II, her life changes more dramatically than she could ever have imagined.

Christine Trent. *The Queen's Dollmaker*. Kensington Books, 2010.
> After barely escaping a fire that killed her father, a famous doll maker, Claudette strikes out on her own as a doll maker and eventually catches the attention of no less than Marie Antoinette.

Salute to Military Fiction

This is one of my favorite displays to do. It works for Memorial Day, it works for the 4th of July, it works for September 11, it works for Veteran's Day, or any other time that your patrons are feeling patriotic.

You can keep this simple with just a really nice display flyer and maybe a small American flag in a stand as a point-of-checkout display. However, if you have some modern or historic military accoutrements, this could look really nice in a display case as well. For the booklist, I've done an author list and noted something about either the branch of the military or the time period in which the authors have set their stories.

Another angle to pursue to enrich your inventory is the wealth of military history and memoir that is available. There are many great books about topics such as the Tuskegee Airmen, the WAVES and the WACs, Roosevelt's Rough Riders, the boy soldiers of the Civil War, and the Native American code talkers. There are also some great modern military memoirs to include such as *Every Man a Tiger* by Tom Clancy, *Lone Survivor* by Marcus Luttrell, and, of course, *Black Hawk Down* by Mark Bowden.

Prop Ideas

American flag

Fatigues

Army boots

Canteen, mess kit, etc.

Related Dewey Subject List

Military History (355)

Revolutionary War (973.3)

War of 1812 (973.52)

Civil War (973.7)

World War I (940.3)

World War II (940.54)

Korean War (951.904)

Vietnam War (959.704)

Gulf Wars (956.7)

History of military weapons (623.4)

History of war photography (778.9)

Related Media

DVDs of any famous war movie (*Saving Private Ryan*, *Platoon*, etc.) or some of the DVDs of cable series such as *Band of Brothers* or *The Pacific*

Notes

Military Fiction Author List

Larry Bond

Bond's <u>First Team</u> books represent not boots-on-the-ground warfare, but instead a war on terror fought with technology. But there are still lots of explosions. Titles include *Edge of War* (Forge, 2010).

Dale Brown

Brown is best-known for his aviation thrillers featuring Air Force navigator Patrick McLanahan. Titles include *Rogue Forces* (William Morrow, 2009).

Stephen Coonts

His best-known series features Rear Admiral Jake Grafton who gets involved with lots of espionage missions and has cool military technology at his disposal. Titles include *The Disciple* (St. Martin's Press, 2009).

Jack Coughlin

A former Marine sniper, Coughlin has written several novels about Gunnery Sgt. Kyle Swanson, a top Marine sniper. Titles include *Clean Kill* (St. Martin's Press, 2009).

Harold Coyle

Coyle is famous for his speculative military fiction about ground warfare. Titles include *Vulcan's Fire* (Forge, 2008).

W. E. B. Griffin

Griffin is an author of military series books including <u>The Brotherhood of War</u> series about the U.S. Army and <u>The Corps</u> series about the Marines. Titles include *The Outlaws* (G. P. Putnam's Sons, 2010).

James W. Huston

A former Navy pilot, Huston's novels include politics, JAG officers, Navy SEALs, and lots of military thrills. Titles include *Falcon Seven* (St. Martin's Press, 2010).

Richard Marcinko

Marcinko, a former Navy SEAL and author of the autobiography *Rogue Warrior*, parlayed his own story into a military action series that bears the same name. Titles include *Rogue Warrior: Seize the Day* (Forge, 2009).

David Poyer

Retired Navy officer Poyer writes nautical military fiction. One series features Navy officer Dan Lenson and another features ex-Coast Guard diver Lyle "Tiller" Galloway. Titles include *The Crisis* (St. Martin's Press, 2009).

Jeff Shaara

Shaara started his career by writing a prequel to his father Michael Shaara's novel *The Killer Angels*. He has since written military fiction from the Revolutionary War to World War II. Titles include *No Less than Victory* (Ballantine Books, 2009).

Satisfy your Sweet Tooth

To get titles for this display, cross fiction with any kind of confection you can think of: candy, sweet, chocolate, doughnuts, ice cream, pastry, pie, cupcake, dessert, and so on. It is interesting to note that there are a large number of erotica fiction books with "chocolate" in the title.

Joanne Fluke writes a great mystery series set in a bakery with titles such as *Carrot Cake Murder* and *Key Lime Pie Murder,* and Diane Mott Davidson writes a series about a murder-solving caterer with many dessert-related titles, such as *Dark Tort* and *Sweet Revenge*. And, don't forget about JoAnna Carl who writes a series subtitled "A Chocoholic Mystery," which includes titles such as *Chocolate to Die for* and *The Chocolate Mouse Trap*. Finally, Sammi Carter writes mysteries set in a candy shop.

Prop Ideas

Baking sheets, muffin tins, pie plates, etc.

Photos or images of pies, cakes, cookies, etc.

Empty boxes of ready-made cookies, pies, ice cream sandwiches, etc.

Candy bar wrappers

Copies of your staff members' favorite cookie or cake recipes

Related Dewey Subject List

Dessert cookbooks (641.86)

History of chocolate (641.3347)

Candy making (641.853)

Related Materials

DVDs of Food Network cooking shows (Alton Brown, Bobby Flay, Rachael Ray, etc.)

Notes

Booklist

Sarah Addison Allen. *The Sugar Queen.* Bantam Dell, 2008.

> Della Lee Baker is on the run from an abusive boyfriend and hides out in Josey Cirrini's closet, a closet that just happens to be full of stashed candy. Suddenly, Della has a mission to turn Josey's life around, whether she likes it or not.

Alan Bradley. *The Sweetness at the Bottom of the Pie.* Delacorte Press, 2009.

> Flavia de Luce is eleven years old when a dead bird on the doorstep of her family's decaying mansion changes her life dramatically.

Nancy Bush. *Candy Apple Red.* Kensington Press, 2005.

> Jane Kelly is a fun, sassy heroine who, when she is not trying to score free drinks, works as a private investigator.

Krista Davis. *Diva Takes the Cake.* Berkley Prime Crime, 2009.

> Sophie Winston, the Domestic Diva, must figure out who killed the groom's ex-wife at her sister's wedding—before she marries him.

Jamie Ford. *Hotel on the Corner of Bitter and Sweet.* Ballantine Books, 2009.

> During a building renovation in Seattle's Chinatown, stored items are discovered that belonged to Japanese residents sent to camps for internment. Henry Lee hears about the incredible find and embarks on a journey of memories that is both bitter and sweet.

Joanne Harris. *Chocolat.* Penguin Books, 1999.

> A newcomer in a French village opens a chocolate shop and has an uncanny ability to cure what ails her customers.

Jen McKinlay. *Sprinkle with Murder.* Berkley Prime Crime, 2010.

> Debut of a mystery series featuring two friends who have just opened a new business: Fairy Tale Cupcakes Bakery.

Ann Pearlman. *The Christmas Cookie Club.* Atria Books, 2009.

> Twelve friends get together in December to share the Christmas cookies they baked and stories about the ups and downs of their year.

Jennifer Ross. *The Icing on the Cupcake.* Ballantine Books, 2010.

> Ansley heads from Dallas to New York after being dumped by her fiancé. She opens a cupcake shop, finds out northern guys are different from southern guys, and discovers that someone wants her shop closed.

Lou Jane Temple. *Death Is Semisweet.* St. Martin's Minotaur, 2002.

> One in a series of mysteries featuring chef Heaven Lee. This one is about a dead man who turns up at the opening of a chocolate factory.

Sew Great

I have a theory: sewing ability skips a generation. I'm the one it skipped. My mother sews, quilts, cross-stitches, knits, and crochets. If it involves needles, thread, and yarn, she does it. I can sew on buttons. Lucky for me my neighbor is a seamstress, and she keeps my pants hemmed for me.

Over the past few years, I've begun to notice a new genre of cozies: those involving knitting, sewing, or crafts. Many of them are series, and not all of them mysteries. Some of them are more what I would call, for lack of a more precise label, women's fiction. Some examples include Marie Bostwick's <u>Cobbled Court Quilt Shop</u> stories and Terri Thayer's quilting mysteries, as well as many of the other authors on the booklist that follows. It goes without saying that my mom enjoys these books since they are right up her alley. Not sure about my neighbor…

Prop Ideas

Sewing implements (scissors, tape measures, bobbins, spools of thread, etc.)

Sewing machine or sewing-machine case

Quilt or afghan squares

Skeins of yarn

Embroidery hoop

Related Dewey Subject List

Sewing (646.2)

Embroidery/cross stitch (746.44)

Quilting (746.46)

Notes

_____

_____

_____

_____

_____

_____

_____

_____

_____

_____

_____

_____

_____

_____

_____

Booklist

Anne Canadeo. *Knit, Purl, Die.* Pocket Books, 2010.
> An installment in the <u>Black Sheep Knitting Club</u> featuring knit shop owner Maggie Messina and her knitting friends.

Elizabeth Lynn Casey. *Death Threads.* Berkley Prime Crime, 2010.
> The members of the Sweet Briar Ladies Society Sewing Circle of South Carolina are not only great seamstresses, they solve crimes as well, led by librarian Toni Sinclair.

Jennifer Chiaverini. *The Aloha Quilt.* Simon & Schuster, 2010.
> One of the Elm Street quilters travels to Hawaii after her divorce to help her friend set up a quilting retreat at a bed and breakfast.

Katharine Davis. *A Slender Thread.* NAL Accent, 2010.
> Margot is devastated when her older sister, a weaver of beautiful textile designs, reveals she is suffering from a rare disease that will rob her of the ability to speak.

Monica Ferris. *Buttons and Bones.* Berkley Prime Crime 2010.
> Betsy Devonshire, owner of the Crewel World needlework shop, also happens to be an amateur detective. This time around, she uncovers a skeleton that reveals the location of a World War II POW camp in northern Minnesota.

Earlene Fowler. *State Fair.* Berkley Prime Crime, 2010.
> An exhibit quilt is stolen and a body discovered at the state fair. Quilter Bennie Harper is up to her ears in mystery, as usual.

Sally Goldenbaum. *Moon Spinners.* New American Library, 2010.
> One of several in Goldenbaum's <u>Seaside Knitters</u> series about crime-solving knitters in a fishing village in Massachusetts.

Ann Hood. *The Knitting Circle.* W. W. Norton, 2007.
> Mary struggles to go on after the sudden death of her young daughter, Stella. When she joins a knitting circle as a distraction from her grief, she discovers its therapeutic quality helps her come back to life.

Kate Jacobs. *The Friday Night Knitting Club.* G. P. Putnam's Sons, 2007.
> A group of friends gather at a tiny knitting shop in Manhattan's Upper West Side each week to swap stories, advice, and knitting tips.

Maggie Sefton. *Skein of the Crime.* Berkley Prime Crime, 2010.
> Part of a mystery knitting series that includes recipes and knitting patterns along with the mysteries.

So Many Books, So Little Time

Almost every reader can relate to the fact that there are just too many good books to read and not enough time to read them. In fact, there are often so many good books on reader lists that they get overwhelmed and forget they even kept a list.

A display by this name could work in several ways. If your fiction shelves get overcrowded, do a point-of-checkout display with popular fiction and put a "So Many Books, So Little Time" flyer next to it. It will probably contain a lot of those kinds of books that readers kept on a list and just never got to read. You could also do a display in which the word "time" appears in the title or the books have a clock on the cover.

Another idea is to use this theme to highlight books about time travel. I'm not much of a science fiction reader, but when I read *Time and Again* by Jack Finney about fifteen years ago, I realized that time travel might be one aspect of SF I could enjoy. Who doesn't want to be transported to another time and place, especially one in which there might be more time to read?

Prop Ideas

Clocks

Watches

Stopwatch

Calendars

Related Dewey Subject List

Time travel/physics (530.11)

Psychology of time (115)

Clock repair (681.113)

Antique clock/watch price guides (739.3075)

Notes

_____

_____

_____

_____

_____

_____

_____

_____

_____

_____

_____

_____

Booklist

John Birmingham. *Weapons of Choice.* Del Rey/Ballantine, 2004.

     The first in the <u>Axis of Time</u> series in which the crew of a mid-twenty-first-century navy battle group goes through a wormhole and ends up in the South Pacific in the middle of World War II.

Michael Crichton. *Timeline.* Alfred A. Knopf, 1999.

     During a time travel experiment, a beloved Yale professor is trapped in medieval France, and a group of his science students follow him back in time to bring him home—as long as the time machine still works, that is.

Seldon Edwards. *The Little Book.* Dutton, 2008.

     Wheeler Burden has already lived a pretty full life when, at forty-seven, he is transported back ninety-one years to Vienna, falls in love, becomes a student of Freud, and meets his war-hero father.

Jasper Fforde. *The Eyre Affair.* Penguin, 2001.

     The first book about literary detective Thursday Next in which she must track down the villain who has his sights set on kidnapping Jane Eyre right out from under Mr. Rochester's nose.

Diana Gabaldon. *Outlander.* Delacorte Press, 1991.

     Jamie, the Scottish Highland hunk, and Claire, the beautiful time-travelling doctor, are the time-travel couple by which all future time travel couples will be measured.

Richard Matheson. *Somewhere in Time.* Tor, 2008.

     Originally titled *Bid Time Return*, this romantic time travel story was made into a movie starring Christopher Reeve. It tells the tale of a screen writer who falls in love with the photo of an actress from the previous century and travels back in time to be with her.

Ian McDonald. *Brasyl.* Pyr, 2007.

     Three characters and multiple plot lines converge across time, where an entrepreneur, a Jesuit missionary, and a television producer inhabit three versions of Brazil.

Audrey Niffenegger. *The Time Traveler's Wife.* Harcourt, 2003.

     Henry is a charismatic librarian married to Clare, a beautiful artist. Can love conquer even Henry's Chrono-Displacement Disorder—a condition that makes him involuntarily travel through time?

H. G. Wells. *The Time Machine.* Penguin, 2005.

     The classic story of the Time Traveler who ventures far into the future and then must find his way back home. As much social commentary as it is science fiction, maybe even more so.

Connie Willis. *To Say Nothing of the Dog.* Bantam Books, 1998.

     Ned Henry is a time traveler hired to research the building of the Coventry Cathedral, destroyed in a Nazi air raid. When fellow traveler Verity Kindle brings along an object from the past, she and Ned must figure out how to set time right.

Speed Reading

Even people who are not interested in NASCAR usually do a double take at this display because it is so colorful. I did it as a point of checkout display once because I needed the nearby power source for the blinking traffic light lamp I used. The photo here shows a small table top display that includes a piece from a toy race-car track. It also shows a portion of the stop sign-shaped rug we had in front of it. If you have a bigger table or low shelf top, you could use more of the track, put some toy cars on it, and even add a finish line.

Books for this display include a surprising number of individual titles having to do with car racing. There is also a NASCAR series written by author Pamela Britton, the <u>Rolling Thunder Stock Car Racing</u> series by Kent Wright and Don Keith, and even a Harlequin romance NASCAR series with a very cute checkered flag spine label detail. In addition, there is a manga series called <u>Initial D</u> that features car racing, written by Shuichi Shigeno, as well as a YA Christian fiction series called <u>RPM,</u> written by Chris Fabry.

Prop Ideas

Checkered flag

Toy car race track

Traffic signs

Racing gear (helmet, jacket, etc.)

Traffic light

"Finish Line" banner

Speed Racer television series action figures

Related Dewey Subject List

NASCAR and auto racing (796.72)

Biographies of famous race car drivers (e.g., Dale Earnhardt)

Car history and repair (629s)

Related Media

DVDs of rereleased *Speed Racer* cartoons

DVDs of episodes of *Driven to Win*, a television series about up and coming NASCAR drivers

Notes

_____

_____

_____

_____

_____

Booklist

Christina Crooks. *Thrill of the Chase.* Five Star, 2007.
> Sarah Matell is the nontraditional heroine of this romance novel—she's a technician in her dad's auto speed shop as well as a drag racing protégé to the handsome new owner.

Janet Evanovich. *Motor Mouth.* HarperCollins, 2006.
> A slapstick thriller starring racing fan Alexandra Barnaby and her NASCAR boyfriend Sam Hooker.

Stephen Hunter. *Night of Thunder.* Simon & Schuster, 2008.
> Set against a week-long NASCAR event in Tennessee, tough Vietnam vet Bob Lee Swagger hunts down drug runners and his daughter's would-be assassin.

Joyce Lavene. *Hooked Up.* Midnight Ink, 2008.
> Part of the Stock Car Racing mystery series in which ex-cop and NASCAR fan Glad Wycznewski finds somebody sleeping in his bed. And that somebody ends up dead.

Erin McCarthy. *Hard and Fast.* Berkley Sensation, 2009.
> This not-so-subtly titled romance features a grad student studying the dating habits of car racers. It isn't long before she crashes headlong into a handsome driver with a dark secret.

Sharyn McCrumb. *Faster Pastor.* Ingalls Publishing Group, 2010.
> A race-car driver wrecks his car in the midst of a Tennessee NASCAR legend's funeral procession and avoids jail by training the local ministers for a big race in the dead driver's honor.

Sharyn McCrumb. *Once Around the Track.* Kensington, 2007.
> An all-female NASCAR pit crew is sponsored by the female version of Viagra—now they just need a driver.

Jenna McKnight. *Love in the Fast Lane.* Avon Books, 2007.
> Legendary (and dead) race car driver Larry Cooper haunts current racing champ Scott Templeton until he agrees to help Cooper's beautiful daughter find his missing classic car.

Ann B. Ross. *Miss Julia Hits the Road.* Viking, 2003.
> The irrepressible Miss Julia won't stand for it when her housekeeper is evicted by a greedy landlord. Along with her boyfriend, Sam, who seems to be having a midlife crisis, she enters a motorcycle marathon to raise money to help her friend.

Garth Stein. *The Art of Racing in the Rain.* HarperCollins, 2008.
> The story of Denny Swift, the aptly named, up-and-coming race-car driver, as told by his dog, Enzo.

Spin-offs

Spin-offs, knockoffs, even rip-offs. Whatever you want to call them, these are famous books whose characters, setting, or plot have been borrowed and repurposed by another author.

Jane Austen books are a favorite target for spin-offs, and there have certainly been some worthy efforts. Pamela Aidan wrote a very nice trilogy from the point of view of Mr. Darcy: *An Assembly Such as This, Duty and Desire*, and *These Three Remain*. Rebecca Ann Collins has also written a series of sequels to *Pride and Prejudice* called <u>The Pemberley Chronicles</u>. Carrie Bebris got into the act with her <u>Mr. and Mrs. Darcy</u> mysteries, while Stephanie Barron pens a series in which Jane herself is the sleuth.

There is also a breed of spin-offs involving classic novels and monsters. *Sense and Sensibility and Sea Monsters* and *Android Karenina* by Ben H. Winters and *Little Women and Werewolves* by Porter Grand are just a few. And, there are books in which the title of the book is a parody of another famous book. Examples include books by Jill Churchill (*The Accidental Florist, Midsummer Night's Scream*, etc.) and Dorothy Cannell (*Withering Heights, The Importance of Being Ernestine*, etc.)

This display works well at point of checkout, and you could put a group of similar spin-offs together, such as the Jane Austen spinoffs listed above or some of the Gregory Maguire books, spun off of Frank Baum's Oz books, such as *Wicked* and *A Lion among Men.*

Prop Ideas

Tops, flying discs, or other spinning toys

Images of tornados, cyclones, and other spinning storm patterns

Related Dewey Subject List

Humorous literary parodies (818s)

Related Media

DVDs of movie versions of the original book, paired with the spin-off book

Notes

_____

_____

_____

_____

_____

_____

_____

_____

_____

_____

_____

Booklist

Joan Aiken. *Mansfield Park Revisited.* Sourcebooks Landmark, 2008.
> A continuation of the original in which Fanny's younger sister Susan moves to Mansfield Park to be Lady Bertram's new companion.

Susan Wittig Albert. *The Tale of Applebeck Orchard.* Berkley Prime Crime, 2009.
> One of Albert's charming mystery tales featuring sleuth Beatrix Potter who is aided by her human and animal friends. This time around, a ghostly arsonist may be at work near her farm.

Sally Beauman. *Rebecca's Tale.* Morrow, 2001.
> Set twenty years after the death of the enigmatic Rebecca, this sequel revisits the characters to see how her demise affected their lives.

Eileen Favorite. *The Heroines.* Scribner, 2008.
> Penny Entwhistle's mother owns a bed and breakfast that caters to popular fictional heroines whose book lives are so hectic they need a vacation.

Laurie R. King. *The Beekeeper's Apprentice.* Picador/Thomas Dunne Books, 2007.
> The introductory Mary Russell novel in which she and Sherlock Holmes meet in a meadow full of bees in Sussex.

Sheila Kohler. *Becoming Jane Eyre.* Penguin Books, 2009.
> Charlotte Brontë's life was nearly as tragic as her famous gothic heroine, Jane Eyre. Here is the story of the novel as well as the story of three talented spinster sisters.

Dean R. Koontz. *Dean Koontz's Frankenstein. Book One, Prodigal Son.* Bantam Books, 2005.
> One of the modern masters of the horror genre, Koontz delivers a retelling of the Frankenstein story set in modern New Orleans, in which an evil scientist plans to replace humanity with his "clones."

Eric Rauchway. *Banana Republican: From the Buchanan File.* Farrar, Straus & Giroux, 2010.
> Tom Buchanan of *The Great Gatsby* discovers that his aunt Gertrude has hold of the family fortune, and when she sends him to Nicaragua to check on investments, he sees his chance to gain control.

Laurie Sheck. *A Monster's Notes.* Alfred A. Knopf, 2009.
> What if Mary Shelley's creation was not an imaginary monster but an immortal creature that followed her throughout her life? This is that creature's notebook.

Sharon Shinn. *Jenna Starborn.* Ace Books, 2002.
> A cool science-fiction retelling of *Jane Eyre* in which a baby harvested from gen-tanks takes a job maintaining nuclear reactors at Thorrastone Park.

From *Ready-Made Book Displays* by Nancy M. Henkel. Santa Barbara, CA: Libraries Unlimited. Copyright © 2011.

Take Me Out to the Ball Game

This is a great display to use in April to coincide with opening day of baseball season, in July during the All-Star Break, or in October during the World Series. You could also put it up in the middle of the summer when your favorite MLB team is on a winning streak.

There is a fair amount of baseball fiction available, including a few classics like *The Natural* by Bernard Malamud and *Shoeless Joe* by W. P. Kinsella. Troy Soos also wrote a series about a player for the Cincinnati Reds who solves murders during the 1919 season. If you need more titles to round out your inventory, there are several authors who write baseball fiction for kids and teens including Carl Deuker, Dan Gutman, Robert Lipsyte, Mike Lupica, and Will Weaver.

Prop Ideas

Baseball uniform accessories (glove, batting glove, cap, batting helmet, catcher's mask, etc.)

Ball

Bat

Bases

Cracker Jack box

Bag of peanuts

Score sheet

Game program

Baseball cards

Related Dewey Subject List

Baseball history/teams/coaching (796.357)

Biography of famous players and/or managers (e.g., Jackie Robinson)

Casey at the Bat (811.52)

Notes

_____

_____

_____

_____

_____

_____

_____

_____

Booklist

Donald Bain. *Three Strikes and You're Dead.* New American Library, 2006.

> This <u>Murder She Wrote</u> novel finds Jessica Fletcher investigating the murder of a minor league baseball player whose bitter rival for the team is also the prime suspect in the crime.

Frank Deford. *The Entitled: A Tale of Modern Baseball.* Sourcebooks, 2007.

> After years of struggling at various levels of baseball, Howie Traveler has finally gotten a job managing the Cleveland Indians. It might all be for naught when his star player, whom he was hired to control and motivate, may be brought up on rape charges.

David James Duncan. *The Brothers K.* Bantam Doubleday Dell, 1992.

> Chronicles the story of the Chance family as they grow up during the 50s and 60s with a father who dreams of a professional baseball career and a mother who hopes to protect her family with increasingly fanatical religious beliefs.

Stephen Frey. *Forced Out.* Atria Books, 2008.

> Jack Barrett is a reluctantly retired Yankee scout. When he attends a minor league game and spots a promising young player, he hopes it is his ticket back to the big leagues. But the troubled young player has secrets, and so does the Mafia hit man who may be after him.

Kevin King. *All the Stars Came Out That Night.* Dutton, 2005.

> King's fiction debut tells the story of a baseball game played just days after the close of the World Series in 1934, between a team of major league stars and a group of black all-stars.

Bernard Malamud. *The Natural.* Farrar, Straus & Giroux, 2003.

> Possibly the most famous baseball novel ever written. *The Natural* tells the story of Roy Hobbs, a man with phenomenal natural baseball talent whose career is derailed and then redeemed many years later.

Howard Frank Mosher. *Waiting for Teddy Williams.* Houghton Mifflin, 2004.

> A lonely kid in a small Vermont town grows up to be a Boston Red Sox star thanks to a drifter who teaches him to play baseball. A fantasy love story written to the game.

Robert B. Parker. *Double Play.* G. P. Putnam's Sons, 2004.

> Joseph Burke, a World War II veteran, is a broken man in many ways when he is hired by the Brooklyn Dodgers to be the body guard for Jackie Robinson, the year he broke the color barrier.

Mary-Ann Tirone Smith. *Dirty Water: A Red Sox Mystery.* Hall of Fame Press, 2008.

> Boston detective Rocky Patel ends up with two cases that will probably turn out to be connected: an abandoned baby left at the Red Sox clubhouse and a badly beaten young woman found near Fenway Park.

Joseph E. Wallace. *Diamond Ruby.* Touchstone, 2010.

> After her family dies in the 1918 flu epidemic, Ruby takes on the raising of her young nieces and discovers she has a talent for throwing a baseball. The story features a tough heroine, lots of Prohibition-era detail, and a brush with Babe Ruth.

Take Note

This display works really well on an endcap. Use empty DVD cases to build little risers so it looks like the books are on a performance stage. You could drape a piece of fabric over the top to simulate a curtain, or you could use sheet music or oversized musical notes as a back drop.

To find titles for the display inventory, do a fiction search combined with the names of various composers, with different musical styles, or even just with the word "music."

Put this display up to celebrate National Music Week in May.

Prop Ideas

Sheet music

Instrument case

Musical notes

Related Dewey Subject List

History of music (780.9)

Musical instruments (784.19)

Notes

Booklist

Laurel Corona. *The Four Seasons.* Voice Hyperion, 2008.

    Venice, Italy, in 1695. Two baby girls are dropped off at an orphanage. Follow their lives as one becomes a famous soloist and one becomes a violinist under the tutelage of Vivaldi.

Stephanie Cowell. *Marrying Mozart.* Viking, 2004.

    Sophie Weber looks back on her life with her sisters when, as young girls, their parents were landlords for Mozart and schemed to marry them all to rich husbands.

Susanne Dunlap. *Emilie's Voice.* Simon & Schuster, 2005.

    It is the beautiful voice of Emilie that lands her at Versailles in the court of Louis XIV. It is the two ambitious women vying for the king's attention that put her in danger.

Rupert Holmes. *Swing.* Random House, 2005.

    The setting is the 1940 World's Fair in San Francisco. When a suicide victim lands at jazz musician Ray Sherwood's feet, he gets caught up in an investigation more sinister than he could have imagined.

Louise Marley. *The Glass Harmonica.* Ace Books, 2000.

    Part science fiction and part historical fiction, this is the story of two young musicians who live over two hundred years apart from each other and can communicate through the playing of their instrument: the glass harmonica.

Alexander McCall Smith. *La's Orchestra Saves the World.* Pantheon Books, 2008.

    A stand-alone novel by the prolific McCall Smith tells the story of Lavender, known as La, and how she organizes an amateur orchestra to help boost morale in an English village during World War II.

Jane Mendelsohn. *American Music.* Alfred A. Knopf, 2010.

    A mesmerizing love story about a wounded Iraq war veteran whose body is the conduit for a symphony of stories heard only by the physical therapist assigned to his case.

Ann Patchett. *Bel Canto.* HarperCollins, 2001.

    American opera singer Roxane Coss is at the heart of this dreamlike novel about a group of international businesspeople who are taken hostage while attending a birthday party for a Japanese industrialist in South Africa.

Andromeda Romano-Lax. *The Spanish Bow.* Harcourt, 2007.

    Feliu Delargo's father leaves him a cello bow that ultimately takes him from the homes of artists to those of royalty and dictators. Through the political and musical turmoil, the one constant is his lifelong friendship and sometimes rivalry with pianist Justo Al-Cerraz.

Mark Salzman. *The Soloist.* Random House, 1994.

    Renne was a child prodigy on the cello until his gift left him as a teen. Now as an adult, his life suddenly changes when he takes on another prodigy as a student and serves on a jury in a murder trial.

Tip Your Hat

Like many of the other displays in this book, this one was born in the stacks. There are books with eyeballs on the cover, books with chairs on the cover, and now, books with hats on the cover. This one takes a little more work to fill the display inventory because the usual keyword search in the catalog comes up with mostly children's books. Gems such as *The 500 Hats of Bartholomew Cubbins* by Dr. Seuss, *Caps for Sale* by Esphyr Slobodkina, and *Old Hat, New Hat* by Jan and Stan Berenstain turned up in the search but may not be exactly what you are looking for.

Prop Ideas

Hats (the more interesting and offbeat, the better)

Hat box

Hat stand

Related Dewey Subject List

Millinery (646.504)

Knitting hats (746.432)

Fashion hats (391.43)

Notes

Booklist

Kurt Andersen. *Heyday.* Random House, 2007.

    The United States is the land of opportunity, and Englishman Benjamin Knowles is going to grab every bit that 1840s America has to offer. Packed with historical events and the fascinating characters who bring them to life, Knowles is in for an adventure.

Mary Kay Andrews. *Deep Dish.* Harper, 2008.

    The Cooking Channel is looking for a fresh new face, and chef Gina Foxton wants the job. Unfortunately, a handsome chef with a wildlife cooking show is her biggest rival.

Andrew Sean Green. *The Confessions of Max Tivoli.* Farrar, Straus & Giroux, 2007.

    The haunting story of a man born in late-nineteenth-century San Francisco whose body starts out old and grows progressively younger. His mother cautions him to live by one rule: be what they think you are.

Min Jin Lee. *Free Food for Millionaires.* Warner Books, 2007.

    Casey Han is the daughter of Korean immigrants. When she graduates from Princeton, she confronts the reality of trying to maintain the lifestyle she was educated to expect.

Donald McCaig. *Rhett Butler's People.* St. Martin's Press, 2007.

    Finally, the backstory of one of literature's most enigmatic figures.

Marsha Moyer. *Return of the Stardust Cowgirl.* Three Rivers Press, 2008.

    The final installment of Moyer's heartwarming <u>Lucy Hatch</u> series in which her husband, Ash, returns home from Nashville to the tiny Texas town of Mooney and is soon followed by Ash's pregnant daughter, a rising country singer seeking to escape a cheating husband.

David Poyer. *Korea Strait.* St. Martin's Press, 2007.

    Seemingly ripped from the headlines, this thriller is one in the series featuring U.S. Navy captain Dan Lenson. This time he is chasing unidentified nuclear subs that may be an invasion force from North Korea.

Naomi Ragen. *The Saturday Wife.* St. Martin's Press, 2007.

    Delilah's goal was always to marry rich. When she instead marries an earnest rabbi and then pushes him to take a job with a wealthy congregation, she finds both her life and her faith will never be the same.

Haywood Smith. *The Red Hat Club.* St. Martin's Press, 2003.

    A feisty group of Southern ladies (who call themselves the Mademoiselles) discover that one of their husbands might be cheating. The red hat club is off to catch him red-handed.

Regina Hale Sutherland. *The Red Hat Society's Acting Their Age.* Warner Vision Books, 2005.

    The first in a series about women of a certain age, in which Mia and Leanne find a runaway teen hiding in their coffee shop, the Brewed Awakening.

Tough Cookies

This is an easy display to do because there are so many great female characters in series novels. There are also a lot of terrific biographies of indomitable women that will supplement this display.

This is a great display to do in March in honor of Women's History Month. Include props of old-fashioned appliances (or photos of them) such as butter churns or water pump handles or photos of women's clothing items from history, such as corsets, giant hats with massive feathers, or tiny Chinese shoes belonging to women with bound feet. There are also a large number of titles shelved in various sections of the 900s dealing with women's roles during an era of history (e.g., nurses in Vietnam, WACs in World War II, female leaders from the medieval period, and travelogues written by intrepid Victorian ladies). You could also pull books of poetry by women or even stories of infamous women of the Bible. There are a lot of tough cookies out there.

For the display in the photo, I went a different route. I had an empty lobby display case that I filled with books featuring tough female characters, and for props I used packages of cookies.

Prop Ideas

Old-fashioned handheld appliances (irons, egg beaters, etc.)

Vintage women's shoes or hats

Packages of cookies

Related Dewey Subject List

Collected biography on women (920.72)

History of cooking (394.10973)

Women's history (305.4)

Women's suffrage (324.623)

Notes

Tough Cookies Author List

Linda Barnes
> *Flashpoint* (St. Martin's, 2008) and *Lie Down with the Devil* (St. Martin's Minotaur, 2008), featuring red-headed private eye Carlotta Carlyle.

Nevada Barr
> *Borderline* (G. P. Putnam's Sons, 2009) and *Burn* (Minotaur Books, 2010), featuring park ranger Anna Pigeon.

Patricia Cornwell
> *Cause of Death* (Berkley Books, 2007) and *Point of Origin* (Berkley Books, 2008), featuring medical examiner Kay Scarpetta.

Janet Evanovich
> *One for the Money* (St. Martin's Griffin, 2006) and *Sizzling Sixteen* (St. Martin's Press, 2010), featuring bounty hunter Stephanie Plum.

Linda Fairstein
> *Hell Gate* (Dutton, 2010) and *Lethal Legacy* (Doubleday, 2009), featuring Assistant District Attorney Alexandra Cooper.

Sue Grafton
> *A Is for Alibi* (St. Martin's Paperbacks, 2005) and *U Is for Undertow* (G. P. Putnam's Sons, 2009), featuring private investigator Kinsey Milhone.

Marcia Muller
> *Burn Out* (Grand Central, 2008) and *Coming Back* (Grand Central, 2010), featuring private investigator Sharon McCone.

Sara Paretsky
> *Body Work* (G. P. Putnam's Sons, 2010) and *Hardball* (G. P. Putnam's Sons, 2009), featuring private investigator V. I. Warshawski.

J. D. Robb
> *Fantasy in Death* (G. P. Putnam's Sons, 2010) and *Indulgence in Death* (G. P. Putnam's Sons, 2010), featuring New York police officer Eve Dallas.

Lisa Scottoline
> *Dead Ringer* (HarperCollins, 2003) and *Lady Killer* (Harper, 2008), featuring the lady lawyers of Rosato and Associates.

Dana Stabenow
> *A Night Too Dark* (Minotaur Books, 2010) and *Whisper to the Blood* (Minotaur Books, 2009), featuring Alaska detective Kate Shugak.

Sarah Strohmeyer
> *Bubbles a Broad* (Dutton, 2004) and *Bubbles Betrothed* (Dutton, 2005), featuring beautician turned sleuth Bubbles Yablonsky.

The Weather Report

You can't predict the weather, but you might be able to predict success with this display. Use an open umbrella as one of your props, and people can't help but come over and see why it's there.

One day I was wandering through the adult fiction stacks and noticed that Rene Gutteridge had three titles in a row on the shelf with the word "storm" in the title: *The Splitting Storm*, *Storm Gathering*, and *Storm Surge*. Later that day, a patron asked whether we had any of Rachel Caine's <u>Weather Warden</u> books, a series about an organization that protects people from climactic weather events and has cool titles like *Heat Stroke* and *Gale Force*. Obviously, I was meant to do a display about weather-related fiction.

It is easy to get titles for this display. Do a keyword search in your catalog for fiction crossed with words like rain, snow, frost, hail, sun, wind, clouds, tornado, and storm, and you will have plenty of titles to work with.

Prop Ideas

Snow boots

Sunglasses

Gloves/mittens/scarf

Sunscreen

Beach towel

Umbrella

Rain hat/boots

Weather satellite map of your region (easily downloaded from the Internet)

Related Dewey Subject List

Weather (551.5)

Global warming (363.73)

Notes

_____

_____

_____

_____

_____

_____

_____

_____

_____

_____

_____

_____

_____

_____

Booklist

Tom Bradby. *The Master of Rain.* Doubleday, 2002.

It is 1926. A young Russian woman is murdered in Shanghai. A young English policeman investigating the crime is dragged deep into the corruption of the city, learning that some crimes are not supposed to be solved.

James Lee Burke. *Rain Gods.* Simon and Schuster, 2009.

Running from his haunted past, Hackberry Holland becomes the new sheriff in a tiny Texas border town and discovers that a murder investigation takes his mind off his own demons.

Liam Callanan. *The Cloud Atlas.* Delacorte Press, 2004.

A novel of love and secrets in which an army sergeant is sent to Alaska during World War II to disarm Japanese rice paper balloon bombs.

Anne Enright. *Yesterday's Weather.* Grove Press, 2008.

A collection of stories set in modern Ireland about ordinary men and women dealing with love, marriage, and family.

David Guterson. *Snow Falling on Cedars.* Vintage Books, 1995.

When Ishmael Chambers returns home as a reporter to an island in Puget Sound after World War II, he finds a heated land dispute related to Japanese internment and a murder possibly committed by the husband of his childhood sweetheart.

Peter Hoeg. *Smilla's Sense of Snow.* Delta Trade Paperbacks, 1993.

Smilla Jasperson decides to investigate the accidental death of her young neighbor, and in the process uncovers some shocking secrets.

Lily King. *Father of the Rain.* Atlantic Monthly Press, 2010.

When Daley's parents divorce, she learns to navigate the vastly different households her parents have created. As an adult, she must decide whether to put her life on hold to save her father.

Dean Koontz. *Lightning.* Berkley Books, 2003.

Koontz's classic about a young girl who is repeatedly saved by a stranger who appears in a bolt of lightning. Then comes the day he demands her help.

Robin McKinley. *Sunshine.* Berkley Books, 2003.

As the daughter of a sorcerer, Rae Seddon, known as Sunshine, is being recruited to become part of the Special Others Forces to combat a vampire takeover. Meanwhile, she is kidnapped by a group of vampires who intend to serve her to their boss for dinner.

Caroline Paul. *East Wind, Rain.* William Morrow, 2006.

On the isolated Hawaiian island of Niihau, a small plane crashes. Only a Japanese American couple living on the island realizes that the pilot has just taken part in the bombing of Pearl Harbor. A novel of love and loyalty.

You Are There

If you've ever read a book and really felt like you came to know the place where it was set, that's a book for the "You Are There" display. Some authors just seem to have a knack for bringing a place alive in their books. Some authors that do this particularly well include Nevada Barr, Larry McMurtry, James Michener, and Annie Proulx. Any books by these authors could fill out your display inventory, and you could also turn to historical fiction, science fiction, and fantasy, since these genres often include strong elements of setting. Another option is to look for books that include the name of a place in the title, such as Larry Watson's *Montana 1948*. Also, any book that includes a map on the endpapers is probably going to fit this display nicely.

To complete this display, include props that evoke a particular place: a small statue of the Eifel Tower, salt and pepper shakers shaped like the Statue of Liberty, a wooden sword from China, a hand-painted plate from Guatemala, or even a pair of plastic mini replicas of the Easter Island statues from a McDonald's Happy Meal.

Prop Ideas

Cloth or blankets with patterns evocative of other countries

Maps

Mini-replicas of famous world landmarks (see above for examples)

Related Dewey Subject List

Travel writing (910s)

Notes

Booklist

David Benioff. *City of Thieves.* Viking, 2008.

      During the dark and hungry siege of Leningrad, a young Jewish man and a Russian army deserter scour the city and the countryside on a seemingly impossible errand for an NKVD colonel.

Pat Conroy. *South of Broad.* Nan A. Talese, 2009.

      Both Charleston, South Carolina, and San Francisco, California, are brought to life in this tale of a diverse group of friends who orbit around their pal, Leo King, whom they lovingly refer to as "the Toad."

Jamie Ford. *Hotel on the Corner of Bitter and Sweet.* Ballantine Books, 2009.

      As Chinese American boy Henry Yee comes of age during World War II, his life revolves around Seattle's Japantown, Sheldon the street musician, and his best friend Keiko.

Barbara Kingsolver. *Prodigal Summer.* HarperCollins, 2000.

      One lush summer brings together the lives of a wildlife biologist, a widowed "bug scientist," and a pair of feuding elderly neighbors all against the backdrop of the mountains and valleys of Appalachia.

Catherine O'Flynn. *What Was Lost.* Henry Holt and Company, 2008.

      A Birmingham, England, shopping mall is the central character in this mystery/ghost story/ romance. When Kurt and Lisa, a security guard and record store manager, see a little girl on surveillance video, they believe it might be the same girl who disappeared at the mall almost twenty years before.

Francine Rivers. *A Voice in the Wind.* Tyndale House, 1993.

      The first book in the <u>Mark of the Lion</u> series begins the story of Hadassah, a Jewish slave girl taken as prisoner to a decadent Rome after the fall of Jerusalem and Atretes, a German kidnapped to fight in the Coliseum as a gladiator.

Carlos Ruiz Zafon. *The Angel's Game.* Doubleday, 2009.

      Zafon, author of *The Shadow of the Wind*, returns to mid-twentieth-century Barcelona for a tale about a young author who is offered a great deal of money to write a book unlike any other.

Edward Rutherford. *New York.* Doubleday, 2009.

      The master of historical epic turns his attention to the Big Apple, covering generations of families, industry, love, and war from the birth of the city to the aftermath of September 11.

Mary Ann Shaffer. *The Guernsey Literary and Potato Peel Pie Society.* Dial Press, 2008.

      A novel in letters between a London World War II correspondent and a group of folks who lived through the German occupation of the Channel Islands.

Kathryn Stockett. *The Help.* Amy Einhorn Books, 2009.

      Told from the point of view of three women as they struggle to negotiate the relationships between class and race in Jackson, Mississippi, in the early 1960s.

From *Ready-Made Book Displays* by Nancy M. Henkel. Santa Barbara, CA: Libraries Unlimited. Copyright © 2011.

Appendix: Displays by Month

	Event	Display Title
January	Mozart's Birthday (January 27)	Take Note
	National Blood Donor Month	Blood Types
	New Year's Day	Grand Openings
	New Year's Day	Read Through the Year
February	National Marriage Week (February 7–14)	Here Comes the Bride
	National Cat Health Month	Curl Up with the Purrfect Book
	Annual Westminster Kennel Club Dog Show	Outside of a Dog
	Valentine's Day	Love and Danger
	Valentine's Day	Satisfy Your Sweet Tooth
March	Bach's Birthday (March 31)	Take Note
	National Bird Watching Month	Books Give You Wings
	Academy Awards	Don't Judge a Book by its Movie
	Louis L'Amour's Birthday (March 22)	Louis L'Amour and More
	Women's History Month	Tough Cookies
	National Doctors' Day (March 30)	Is There a Doctor in the House?
April	National Library Week (mid-April)	Books about Books
	Opening day of baseball season	Take Me Out to the Ball Game
	National Humor Month	Just for Laughs
	Shakespeare's Birthday (April 23rd)	Much Ado about the Bard
	National Dance Week (end of April)	Let's Dance
	National Foot Health Awareness Month	Put Your Best Foot Forward
	Federal income taxes due (April 15)	Reading Makes Cents
May	Kentucky Derby (1st Saturday in May)	Everything Equine
	Mother's Day	It's All Relative
	National Music Week (1st week of May)	Take Note
	Beginning of spring	Books in Bloom
	Memorial Day	Salute to Military Fiction
	Start of boating season	Adventure on the High Seas
	National Healthy Eyes Month	The Eyes Have it
	National Salad Month	Read a Variety of Fruits and Vegetables

Event		**Display Title**
June	Father's Day	It's All Relative
	National Adopt-a-Cat Month	Curl Up with the Purrfect Book
	National Fresh Fruit and Vegetable Month	Read a Variety of Fruits and Vegetables
July	Independence Day (July 4)	Salute to Military Fiction
	Summer weddings	Here Comes the Bride
	National Ice Cream Month	Satisfy Your Sweet Tooth
August	Midsummer	In the Good Old Summertime
	Gene Roddenberry's Birthday (August 19)	Boldly Go
	Wizard of Oz movie anniversary (August 12)	Follow the Yellow Book Road
	International Clown Week (1st week of August)	Just for Laughs
September	First day of school	It's Academic
	National Fall Hat Month	Tip Your Hat
	National Sewing Month	Sew Great
	International Literacy Day (September 8)	Books About Books
October	National Chiropractic Health Month	Back in Circulation
	National Adopt-a-Dog Month	Outside of a Dog
	Halloween	Satisfy Your Sweet Tooth
	World Series	Take Me Out to the Ball Game
November	Veteran's Day	Salute to Military Fiction
	National Education Week (mid-November)	It's Academic
	National Bible Week (week of Thanksgiving)	Biblical Proportions
	Bram Stoker's Birthday (November 8)	Blood Types
	Election Day	Elect to Read
December	Beethoven's Birthday (December 16)	Take Note
	Christmas	Satisfy Your Sweet Tooth

Index

Titles with complete annotations included in this book are denoted in bold type. Titles with just a mention, but no annotation, are denoted in regular type.

About the Author

Photo by Josh Henkel.

NANCY M. HENKEL has worked as a children's librarian, a teen librarian, a school librarian, and as a managing librarian. She has published articles in the *Journal of Youth Services in Libraries and Young Adult Library Services*. In addition, she holds the rank of 5th Degree Black Belt Master Instructor in Tae Kwon Do and is a contributing writer for *Martial Arts Success Magazine*.

33450952R00114

Made in the USA
Lexington, KY
27 June 2014